G.I. Joe or Anne of Green Gables?

Friendly Fire between Canada and the States

Published by ECW PRESS
2120 Queen Street East, Suite 200, Toronto, Ontario, Canada M4E 1E2

NATIONAL LIBRARY OF CANADA CATALOGUING IN PUBLICATION DATA

Gould, Allan, 1944-
G.I. Joe or Anne of Green Gables? : friendly fire between
Canada and the States / Allan Gould.

ISBN 1-55022-602-9

1. Canada—Humor. 2. United States—Humor. 3. Canadian wit and humor (English) I. Title

PS8563.O8438H68 2003   C818'.5402   C2003-902416-4 PR9199.3.G653H68 2003

The publication of *G.I. Joe or Anne of Green Gables?* has been generously supported by the Canada Council, the Ontario Arts Council, and the Government of Canada through the Book Publishing Industry Development Program. Canadä

DISTRIBUTION
CANADA: Jaguar Book Group

UNITED STATES: Independent Publishers Group, 814 North Franklin Street, Chicago, Illinois 60610

PRINTED AND BOUND IN CANADA

ECW PRESS
ecwpress.com

Contents

I wish to thank my wife (of 35 years) Merle, for her patience, guidance, and keenly insightful commentary upon, and early editing of, this book. There should be a Governor General's Award for Being Married to a Freelance Author/Journalist.

And I dedicate this book to my son Judah, his magnificent new bride Shoshana, and my daughter Elisheva, each of whom has experienced the best of both Anne of Green Gables AND G.I. Joe, in their travels and careers. Sure, I could have created this book without them, but it would mean so much less to me. Their lives are my greatest joy.

ACKNOWLEDGEMENTS

Thank you to Cary Fagan, a fine novelist (his *Animal's Waltz* is one of the sweetest, most entertaining books I've read in years), for editing and organizing my text so professionally and wittily; indeed, some of the best gags in this book are his.

And to Jack David, the publisher of ECW PRESS, who supported this U.S./Canada project with great enthusiasm and eagerness from the very beginning; now that I think of it, it was his idea. To say that I couldn't have done it without you, Jack, would be a very serious understatement, sort of like my gags about Canada having dozens of men and women in its armed forces.

And to Leonard Wise, with whom I recently wrote/published *Toronto Street Names*, a wildly successful book. He approached me many years ago with a very, very funny idea: "Don't Leave Home," a book concept which would warn all travelers not to do it, but rather stay at home, lie in their tub, and have a neighbour come over and kick sand into their faces. We worked on it for weeks, developed a marvelous outline and sample chapters but no publisher ever bit. (The fools.) Meanwhile, along came 9/11, and traveling really did become frightening. So I borrowed some of the best ideas and one-liners from that long-ago-abandoned book idea, and Leonard was the man behind many of the finest gags. Thanks to you, too, LW.

And to my parents, Anne and Earl Gould, both long dead, for having left the hell-hole that was then Toronto in the early 1930s (one does not pass up five bucks a day at Ford) and moved to Detroit. There I was born, grew up, and attended grade school, high school, and university, before eventually finding my way to Canada in 1968 with my new, Canadian-born wife Merle. Having dual citizenship, and having split much of my 59 years between the two countries, provided countless advantages to me as a satirist. As the twig is bent, a famous non-Canadian once wrote. And as this book shows, I still am.

INTRODUCTION:
CAUGHT BETWEEN IRATE
AND A COLD PLACE

Canadians understand choices. Do I vote Liberal or Liberal? Do I refuse to purchase the *Globe and Mail* or the *National Post* — and on principle or merely because I am broke due to federal and provincial and municipal taxes that are higher than the Neilson ratings of the latest reality show from the United States? Should I put on long johns and two toques this morning or finally move to Vancouver, where I merely have to choose between raincoats?

But let's jump back a few years and consider the choice that we — or our parents or grandparents — had to make. Would it be Canada or the United States?

It was the choice that made us into Canadians. Perhaps our beloved ancestors (or even we ourselves) didn't think it through very clearly. After all, there may have been just a little stress involved. Here are some possible conditions under which this all-important choice was made:

- You are about to be drafted into the Czarist/Prussian/ Albanian/Nigerian/(name any other) army, yet you strongly disagree with the murderous politics of said regime. Also, you are filled with a selfish longing to keep your arms and legs attached to your torso.

● You are rapidly running out of potatoes, and the bloody Brits won't leave you alone, and you're sick and tired of writing brilliant poetry and majestic theatre while getting drunk all the time.

● You are getting awfully tired of your next-door neighbours bursting into your home at all hours of the day and night, setting fire to your bed, raping your wife, and murdering your children while you wonder wistfully, "There must be more to life than this."

● You hear rumours about the Bering Strait — or whatever it was called a few thousand years ago — being particularly well frozen this winter and decide to make the trek into what will some day be called "North America" and try your luck out there.

● You have been given an actual choice: being drawn and quartered, lynched, starved to death, or shot at dawn. Then you hear that there may be a visa to North America available somewhere in your home and native village.

The question was, a visa to which country? As you hold this book in your typically rough and chafed Canadian hands (from all that drawing of water and hewing of wood), you know the answer, don't you? We or our parents or grandparents or distant forebears chose Canada, or what would become the Dominion of Canada, a promising young nation that would eventually put most of the descendants of those lucky first guys and gals who made it across the Bering Strait thousands of years ago into ill-heated igloos and ever-shrinking reserves. How could they have guessed that there would someday (the 1880s, to be precise) be a Bering Sea dispute in which the U.S. government would begin to seize

Canadian sealing vessels? Yes, even back then, there were ugly tensions between these Usually Friendly Neighbours.

Today, thank God, Jesus, Allah, and Buddha, Canada and the United States are now the closest of friends and allies, eagerly sharing immigrants (if mainly north to south), happily trading softwood lumber, joyfully sending *Time Canada* to homes across this country (whereas we are unsure of what to do with our old copies of *Maclean's*), and endlessly downloading Céline and Britney on both sides of the border, while wondering what each country did to deserve this.

If you are a new immigrant to Canada, or the child or grandchild of one, then you must remember why you chose this beautiful, spacious, tolerant land. You couldn't get into the United States, could you? *Could* you? ADMIT IT.

What all of us living in Canada know is that there are many basic, big, cardinal, central, consequential, critical, essential differences between these two Great Lands — we're just too damn polite to name them. Besides, we know that we needn't feel inferior to our Giant Good Neighbour to the South, but since we actually believe that self-deprecation is a good quality, it's easy.

In reality, though, it's absurd to feel inferior to the United States, even if that other country has ten times the population and a billion times more power and money. So, if we as Canadians ever start to feel petty jealousy toward that loud, exciting, dynamic, wealthy country just to the south of us, we ought to remember just one fact.

Canada is much, much bigger. And size really does count. It must. We get a dozen penile and breast enlargement spams a day.

The grand purpose of this book (destined to win the Governor General's Literary Award, the Giller Prize, or the Herb Apkowitz Memorial Trophy — Canada has a lot of literary awards) is to unveil the real differences between the United States and Canada as well as to show our many common traits. By doing so, I hope to improve a relationship that has grown all too touchy in recent days. At the same time, I hope to give a boost to our long-suffering Canadian egos. So sit back, open a cold one, and start to feel good about yourself.

And, hey, if you need a break after a while, you can always turn on CNN.

PART 1

First Things First:
Language, History, and Fame

THE GOULDSTER'S CANADIAN-AMERICAN DICTIONARY: OR, "WHAT WE HAVE HERE IS A FAILURE TO COMMUNICATE"

Most of us are aware of the minor variations in the way that Canadians and Americans use some words and spell others. For example, take the words *serviette* and *napkin*. A Canadian would use a serviette to mop up any beer that he or she has spilled on a bridge table. An American would use a napkin to mop up the blood after an unfortunate accident with the family gun collection. But there are more profound differences between Canadian and American English, of course, and the meanings of similar words or expressions — whether spelled with a *u* or not — are often remarkably dissimilar.

To avoid further embarrassing and even dangerous misunderstandings, I provide here a compact American-Canadian dictionary.

AMERICAN ENGLISH

American Dream: The right and even obligation of every person who immigrates to or is born in the United States of America to achieve fame, fortune, and a trophy wife less than half the age of the first, after he accomplishes the first two goals.

CANADIAN ENGLISH

Canadian Dream: To pay a serviceman cash in order to avoid the GST; to go to Hawaii (if one lives in British Columbia), Arizona (if one lives on the Prairies), or Florida (if one lives in Ontario, Quebec, or the Maritimes) in winter; and to be able to move to the United States and make real dollars.

AMERICAN ENGLISH

gun control: A communist plot to take away one's constitutional right to bear arms.

CANADIAN ENGLISH

gun control: A communist plot to take away one's God-given right to bear arms (rural usage); a reasonable way for governments to take guns out of the hands of unstable country hicks (city usage).

CANADIAN ENGLISH

violence: What one sees on television every night.

AMERICAN ENGLISH

violence: What one sees outside one's window every day/night.

CANADIAN ENGLISH

Group of Seven: A phrase referring to a number of Canadian artists who joined loosely together in 1920 and proclaimed themselves both modern and Canadian.

AMERICAN ENGLISH

Group of Seven: A global economic term referring to seven major noncommunist powers that have been meeting at formal summits since 1975. In reality, the term should refer to six powers (United States, Great Britain, Germany, France, Italy, and Japan), but out of the biblical injunction to "be kind to dumb creatures" Canada has also been included.

CANADIAN ENGLISH

takeover: To purchase something, as in "Company X was involved in a friendly takeover of Business Y yesterday, affecting both stocks negatively."

AMERICAN ENGLISH

takeover: What the U.S. government must do in order to protect the world and its own interests from aggression, fanaticism, and anti-American actions, as in "By 2006, the forcible takeover of Iraq, North Korea, Iran, Saudi Arabia, Syria, and Alberta (a province in Canada) was accomplished with ease and almost no fatalities, except from occasional 'friendly fire.'"

CANADIAN ENGLISH

French: One of the two official languages of Canada.

AMERICAN ENGLISH

French: A wine-guzzling European people of dubious moral character due to a penchant for wasting time in cafés, surrendering rather than fighting, and refusing to vote with the United States at the United Nations.

CANADIAN ENGLISH

Spanish: Language spoken in Spain and, slightly differently, in Mexico and most of Central and South America.

AMERICAN ENGLISH

Spanish: Language that may not be taught in schools in over a dozen U.S. states lest it undermine the patriotism of Hispanics.

CANADIAN ENGLISH

Liberal: Name of the official ruling federal party in Ottawa, save for brief interregnums over the past century.

AMERICAN ENGLISH

Liberal: Communist; bleeding heart; pro-abortion; anti-school prayer; do-gooder; fur hater; anti-smoking fanatic; Darwinian.

CANADIAN ENGLISH

Adult: A person or animal that has reached maturity either physically or mentally.

AMERICAN ENGLISH

Adult: An adjective informing someone that the movie, videotape, or DVD he or she is about to watch includes hard-core sex.

CANADIAN ENGLISH

Argue: To talk with someone about things you do not agree on.

AMERICAN ENGLISH

Argue: To fight; vehemently disagree; quarrel angrily; reach for your weapon of choice.

CANADIAN ENGLISH

Blade: The metal piece on the bottom of a skate.

AMERICAN ENGLISH

Blade: The flat, sharp part of a knife, often carried in a concealed location.

CANADIAN ENGLISH

Change: When something becomes different.

AMERICAN ENGLISH

Change: Something intolerable, dangerous, evil, or contrary to the Constitution of the United States.

OUR COUNTRY
THEN AND NOW

With age comes maturity (and sometimes premature senility). To gain some perspective on just how far this great country of ours has come, I present the following historical tidbits for your consideration.

THEN	NOW
Mel Hurtig publishes *THE CANADIAN ENCYCLOPEDIA* and goes broke doing it.	Mel Hurtig has his book *THE VANISHING COUNTRY* published for him and has a best-seller at last.
JOHN TURNER and ED BROADBENT fight passionately against BRIAN MULRONEY'S push for a free-trade deal.	Nobody talks about the dangers of free trade anymore except for Mel Hurtig and a few dozen others.
PETER JENNINGS reads the news on Canadian television and makes $100 a week.	Peter Jennings anchors ABC National News for $10 million a year. (U.S.)

THEN	NOW
MARGARET ATWOOD publishes *The Circle Game*, a poetry collection that wins the Governor General's Literary Award, sells dozens of copies, and makes enough money for her to be able to afford contact lenses.	Margaret Atwood wins the Booker Prize, sells countless copies of her books, and is able to afford a modest home in midtown Toronto.
PIERRE TRUDEAU destroys the Canadian economy, alienates the West, and by invoking the War Measures Act turns the whole nation into a banana republic— but without the good weather.	Pierre Trudeau dies and is given a Churchill-like funeral; the entire country mourns for months; his son considers entering federal politics before the Canadian economy gets too good again.
MICHAEL J. FOX appears on Vancouver TV in a Canadian situation comedy and is paid $650 a week.	Michael J. Fox appears on *SPIN CITY*, an American network sit-com, earns $650,000 U.S. a week, and takes out American citizenship.
CANADA lacks any kind of federally sponsored medical care, and people die like flies in their beds at home.	Canadians proudly have universal medical care and die in hospital corridors like flies, waiting for beds.

THEN	NOW
JEAN CHRÉTIEN arrives in Ottawa not knowing more than a few words in English.	Jean Chrétien finishes his third full term as prime minister of Canada not knowing more than a few words in English. Or French.
Canadians watch GUY LOMBARDO on American TV and wonder how he made it, lacking talent.	Canadians watch PAMELA LEE ANDERSON on Baywatch and know that she could not have made it, lacking implants.
The FEDERAL NEW DEMOCRATIC PARTY holds the balance of power in Ottawa along with the Liberals.	The federal NDP holds power meetings in an Ottawa phone booth, once the federal Tories are done with it.
AMERICANS bitch over their dollar being worth only 97¢ against the Canadian dollar when they fly north to ski.	CANADIANS bitch over their dollar being worth only 65¢ against the American dollar when they drive south to swim.
The PARTI QUÉBÉCOIS wins provincial elections and demands "sovereignty-association" with the rest of Canada.	ALL OF CANADA gives up its sovereignty for a trade association with the United States.

THEN	NOW
CANADIANS help to win World War I and World War II.	Canada purchases British subs that sink and cannot return to the surface.
JOHN A. MACDONALD runs Canada while drunk.	RALPH KLEIN of Alberta and *GORDON CAMPBELL* of British Columbia run their provinces and a car in Hawaii while drunk.
Canada witnesses giant Protestant ORANGE DAY PARADES in major cities across the country, offending and frightening millions of Catholics.	Canada's Annual Orange Day Parade in Regina is called off when the other member falls ill.
Millions of Canadian citizens are in an uproar over possible cruise missile testing by the United States over Alberta, even though there is little intelligent life there anyway.	Millions of Canadian citizens are in an uproar over CBC TV's possibly dropping Don Cherry's sidekick on *Hockey Night in Canada*.

Pax Americana/Pox Canadiana

With the obviously unavoidable and inevitable war in Iraq in the spring of 2003, politicians and writers around the world began to speak about "Pax Americana." But then, in early April 2003, even more people around the globe started to refer to "Pox Canadiana" when they spoke of severe acute respiratory syndrome.

NATIVE LAND:
OR,
WHERE WERE YOU BORN, ANYWAY?

Does being born in Canada make a difference? Or within the fifty states of the United States?

Being born on the U.S. side of the border back in the 1960s and 1970s made millions of American teenagers rather uncomfortable during the Vietnam War, which led to tens of thousands of them making sure, a few marriages and years later, that their children would be born on the Canadian side. But is genius, talent, or inspiration limited to north or south of the forty-ninth parallel? As a way of testing the above question, I suggest these speculative examples.

MICKEY SENIOR: If Walt Disney's father had stayed on his family farm in Ontario instead of moving down to the United States, his son would have become a multimillionaire anyway, not by farming but simply by selling the dump when the suburbs of Toronto swallowed up the land.

SNOWBIRD: If Anne Murray had been born in North Carolina instead of Nova Scotia, she would not have had to travel so far to Nashville in order to be discovered up in Canada.

MOGUL: If Jerry Bruckheimer, Hollywood producer extra-ordinaire (*Top Gun, Flashdance, Con Air, Armageddon, Pearl Harbor, Kangaroo Jack*), had been born in Windsor, Ontario, instead of Detroit, Michigan, he would have ended up making movies about dysfunctional farm families (or dysfunctional East Coast fishing families or dysfunctional inner-city Toronto families) with the full financial backing of TeleFilm Canada and the CBC and many Oshawa dentists seeking tax write-offs. On the positive side, nothing would have been blown to bits.

Momma's Boy: If Mackenzie King, who ended up being reelected many times as the prime minister, had been born in the United States instead of this country, he would have been institutionalized.

THE RIGHT STUFF: If Barbara Frum had been born in Niagara Falls, New York, instead of Niagara Falls, Ontario, her son may have had the chance to grow up and write speeches for the president of the United States.

Oh, right, he did that anyway. Must remember to file him under *Apple pie, more American than.*

PART 2

Symbols:
Official and Otherwise

NATIONAL EMBLEMS

THE AMERICAN BALD EAGLE

The bald eagle — or, as it is warmly called by every American citizen above the age of five, *Haliaeetus leucocephalus* — can be found on the backs of American gold coins, the silver dollar, the half dollar, and the quarter and is painted on planes bombing a country near you, even as I type these words. It can also be found on the "Great Seal" of the United States, one seal that no Canadian should ever risk clubbing to death, on videotape or even unseen, if he knows what's good for him.

The eagle has been the national emblem of the United States since 1782, when the country's Great Seal was adopted. In the original drawing, the magnificent bird holds an olive branch in its right talon and a bundle of thirteen arrows in its left talon. Several Republican attempts for a budget increase to fifty arrows have so far been blocked by Democrats questioning the viability of arrow technology.

The bald eagle can be found over most of North America; in fact, one out of every three of these majestic creatures lives in British Columbia, a detail that Canadians are reluctant to mention for fear of reprisal. Instead, we prefer to call them Canadian eagles with a moulting problem.

Naturally, as might be expected from a symbol chosen by the United States, the eagle represents freedom. The bird's very living habits capture that powerful image: bald eagles live on the peaks of high mountains, have sharp pinions, and can fly over valleys for long periods without refuelling. However, if the bald eagle did need oil, Iraq would have been invaded many years earlier. Because they are so huge, bald eagles are not fearful of threats from other birds, unless they are North Korean. Interestingly, bald eagles are frequently harried by smaller birds that, like lone terrorists, can sometimes outmanoeuvre the more powerful creature. This is why the bald eagle, like the American president, is so often in a foul mood.

THE CANADIAN BEAVER

The beaver, on the other hand, is Canada's largest rodent and cannot fly. Its proper name is *Castor Canadensis*, a fact known by hundreds of proud Canadian Latin teachers and biologists. As even those men and women are unaware, this national emblem has influenced the history of Canada more than any other animal, with the possible exception of Moses Znaimer.

For instance, in the early seventeenth century, Champlain pushed westward for the specific purpose of extending the beaver trade. Radisson and Des Groseilliers travelled from Lake Superior to James Bay about 1660, long before the first Liberal ran this country, chiefly to trade in beaver pelts. And countless men (there were no women then) from Montreal, called "the Nor'westers," hunted far across the country in search of beaver.

Like our Friendly Neighbour to the South with its bald eagle, Canadians have put the beaver on coins, stamps, and T-shirts — not bad for a rodent. The beaver enjoys several qualities that Canadians think of as their own. It is a fine swimmer. It is capable of staying underwater for up to a quarter of an hour. When alarmed, it slaps the surface of the water to warn others to take refuge underwater. These instincts remind us of our recent peacekeeping past, before we became a warrior nation, carrying the backpacks and lighter weapons of the U.S. Armed Forces.

The beaver is truly Canadian in other ways. It inhabits forested regions, yet it is rarely found on the Prairies. It builds homes of logs, sticks, mud, and debris. The entrance to its home is underwater (a nod to Vancouver, obviously). It collects wood and fells trees. It builds canals, even if most ships are now too large to get through them. It has small, beady eyes, like many Canadian lawyers and TV producers.

In some ways, the beaver is a more stalwart Canadian than the rest of us. It does not hibernate but copes with the winter, never trying to book a last-minute discount flight to Florida. Fascinatingly, like the vast majority of adult Canadians, the beaver breeds for only a few weeks after each new year and gives birth to no more than two to four babies. (Québécois are an anomaly, however. While they have only 1.1 children on average, their period of copulation is significantly longer. Montreal really is a fun town.)

In earlier times, the beaver, pursued by money-hungry invaders from the Atlantic to the Pacific, nearly became extinct, much like the American bald eagle. However, it thrives now that the beaver hat is out of fashion and the beaver coat is considered a politically despicable sign that the wearer does not consider rodents to be adorable. While there have been attempts to introduce the beaver jockstrap, it has caught on only in Winnipeg.

Writer Margaret Atwood, a Canadian emblem in her own right, loves to note that the beaver has been known to bite off its own testicles and offer them to an enemy when frightened. Most Canadians prefer to simply hand over their uranium, water, and fishing rights.

SOME THOUGHTS ON THE EMBLEMS OF THE TWO NATIONS

It is worth noting that all Canadians appear to be happy with the beaver as our national emblem. Not so with Americans and the bald eagle. Benjamin Franklin, perhaps the greatest American figure of all time (with the possible exception of John Kenneth Galbraith, who is actually Canadian), felt passionately that the eagle was a rotten choice as America's national emblem. I quote without permission since Franklin's touching words have been in the public domain for over two centuries:

"I wish that the bald eagle had not been chosen as the representative of our country. He is a bird of bad moral character, he does not get his living honestly. You may have seen him perched on some dead tree, where, too lazy to fish for himself, he watches the labor of the fishing-hawk, and when that diligent bird has at length taken a fish, and is bearing it to its nest for the support of its mate and young ones, the bald eagle pursues him and takes it from him. Besides, he is a rank coward; the little kingbird, not bigger than a sparrow, attacks him boldly and drives him out of the district. . . . For a truth, the turkey is in comparison a much more respectable bird, and withal a true original native of America. . . ."

In other words, while the beaver may be a rodent, the bald eagle is no turkey.

OUR TWO NATIONAL ANTHEMS

"THE STAR SPANGLED BANNER"

The words of the American anthem, belted out patrioti-
cally at every baseball game, lynching, and church service
across the United States, were written, as every Yankee
schoolchild knows, by Francis Scott Key. He was a young
Washington attorney who had sailed to the British fleet to
obtain the release of a captured American during the War
of 1812. Many think it ironic that his name was Key considering that it is actually physically impossible to sing the
American national anthem on key.

Detained by the British aboard the ship, Key was forced
to witness the bombardment of Fort McHenry near
Baltimore during the night of September 13, 1814. The fort
withstood the attack — thanks to the command of Major
George Armistead, a name on the lips of every American
child from kindergarten on — and the sight of the American
flag still flying at dawn inspired the verses of Key's poem,
which Key wrote on the way back to shore that morning.
Some musicologists believe that, if the waves had not been so
choppy that day, it might have made more sense.

Key's poem was put to an old drinking song, which
seems fitting; alcohol makes "The Star Spangled Banner"

almost possible to sing. The original flag that so moved the young man became one of the many holy icons of the American people. It stayed in the Armistead family for generations, and some of it was cut up as souvenirs, sort of like chunks of wood from the original cross. The remainder of the flag is now safely housed at the National Museum of American History in Washington, DC, and the various pieces cut off over the decades are available on eBay, in the great tradition of American capitalism.

Key's little ditty did not become the official national anthem until President Wilson put through an executive order confirmed only after an act of Congress in 1931, when America's federal politicians were busy becoming isolationist in case another war might come along. (Did they really have to save Europe again? Sigh.) To this day, the lyrics of "The Star Spangled Banner" are imprinted on the mind of every American. As for singing it, Americans shouldn't feel bad; even Shania Twain can't get the tune right. But ask any American, and he or she can rattle off the final words of Francis Scott Key's unforgettable poetry: *"Play ball!"*

"O CANADA"

Canadians, as always, act with much more alacrity and passion when it comes to patriotic matters. "O Canada" was first sung in 1880, and it took only one century — until July 1, 1980 — for it to be proclaimed the country's national anthem. The music, as not a single child in Canada knows (except that little nerd who wrote a grade four report on it for Our Lady of Perpetual Mercy and Guilt in Guelph, Ontario), was composed by Calixa Lavallée, a well-known composer at the time, at least to his immediate family. He wrote the music for a French-language poem by Sir Adolphe-Basile Routhier.

The song gained steadily in popularity despite never having been recorded by either Enrico Caruso or Avril Lavigne. Many English versions were written over the years, the official one originating with Mr. Justice Robert Stanley Weir in 1908, when Canadians were getting revved up to die like flies in the Great War, having just cut their teeth on the Boer War. (God but we loved England back then.) Interestingly, while the official English version includes changes recommended in 1968 by a special joint committee of the Senate and the House of Commons (the Canadian parliamentary system tries to avoid wasting time on such things as education or health care), the French lyrics have remained unaltered to this day. And unknown outside Quebec. Inside Quebec too. Especially.

Unlike the American national anthem, "O Canada" was not dashed off as just another patriotic song by an obscure music teacher. Lavallée was actually known during his lifetime as "Canada's national musician," even though his fiddling was less than expert. It was because he was so popular that he was formally asked to compose music for Routhier's poem. Lavallée was born in Lower Canada in 1842, played with his organ in the cathedral for years without going blind, and actually moved to the United States, where he did a lot better and gained a lot more respect (paving the way for Paul Anka, Joni Mitchell, and Céline Dion). He joined the Northern army during the American Civil War, composed operettas and a symphony, and then reluctantly returned to Canada, where he had nothing better to do than compose "O Canada."

The occasion? Le Congres national des Canadiens-Français, held in 1880, the same time as the St. Jean-Baptiste Day celebrations, a sort of French Canadian version of the Orange Day Parade, except in this case it was the Protestants who were threatened and yelled at.

Lavallée made a number of drafts, determined to create something just as impossible to sing as "The Star Spangled Banner," already number one with a bullet down in the States (they were violent even back then). It is reported that, in the excitement of his great success, Lavallée rushed to show his music to the lieutenant governor, who had commissioned it, without even stopping to sign the manuscript. Of such charming anecdotes are dull reports made by grade school students over a century later.

The first performance of "O Canada" took place on June 24, 1880, at a banquet in Quebec City, with French words that no anglophone has ever taken the trouble to learn. It was well received but, like so many Canadian institutions and events, promptly forgotten by everyone except Pierre Berton.

It is telling that, in the 1891 obituary of Lavallée, no mention was made of "O Canada" as being among his accomplishments — surely the result of traditional Canadian modesty. Nor was the future national anthem noted in a biography of Judge Routhier published in 1898. English Canada likely did not hear "O Canada" until a group of school children sang it for the Duke and Duchess of Cornwall (later King George V and Queen Mary), touring Canada in 1901 to the thrill of millions of native-born citizens and the utter lack of interest from the millions of immigrants pouring into the country at that time.

Over the years, there have been many attempts by English-speaking poets and versifiers — make that just versifiers — to create the definitive lyrics for "O Canada." In 1906, a Toronto doctor named Thomas Bedford Richardson wrote one version. In 1908, a certain Mercy E. Powell McCulloch (voted "the most gentile name in human history" by the Kingston, Ontario, B'nai B'rith) wrote another version that also did not take. A version also written in 1908, by Robert Stanley Weir, a lawyer and recorder of the city of Montreal, finally had staying power. It was published in an official form for the diamond jubilee of Confederation in 1927 and has lasted until this day, give or take a few words.

As for Lavallée, like most Canadians (especially Maritimers), he ended up moving to Boston, where he became impoverished and sick, dying at the age of forty-nine in 1891. Had he only lived to see "O Canada" sung proudly, if rarely correctly, before violent hockey games to this very day, it probably would have made no difference to him whatsoever.

A SCHOLARLY STUDY OF
THE AMERICAN NATIONAL ANTHEM
by Carolyn Parrish, Liberal Member of Parliament, and Robert Fulford, Critic and Columnist, the *National Post*

Oh, say can you see,

Ms. Parrish: "This is just one more example of American vanity: 'can *you* see' it asks us. Clearly, in their warped and diseased minds, only *Yankees* can truly 'see' anything."

Mr. Fulford: "A fine example of American generosity and sensitivity to the feelings of a minority. Originally 'Jose, can you see,' this clearly refers to the growing number of Hispanics gathered to the bosom of America when large chunks of Mexico were welcomed to become part of Texas."

By the dawn's early light,

Ms. Parrish: "As if it only 'dawns' on *them.* It also looks as if the damned Yankees are claiming the discovery of standard time as well with this line, when, as every Canadian schoolchild knows, that extraordinary concept was developed by Canada's own Sir Sandford Fleming, who also worked on our great national railway and invented our country's first postage stamp. Maybe the Americans will claim those too?"

Mr. Fulford: "A poetic image, referring to the difficulty with which Mr. Francis Scott Key struggled to spot the American flag in the distance. Few Canadian poets were writing such quality verse at this early date."

What so proudly we hailed at the twilight's last gleaming?

Ms. Parrish: "This line really doesn't make any sense at all, sort of like American foreign policy under the morons in Washington, DC, today. Note the superpatriotic word 'proud'; we Canadians are never too proud about anything, which probably keeps us away from attacking other countries every few minutes. As for 'twilight's last gleaming,' I'm clueless about that phrase — although I think it was the title of an idiotic Hollywood film of a few years ago: violent and brain dead, as always."

Mr. Fulford: "Note the lovely weather images: 'hail,' 'twilight,' 'gleaming.' This is nineteenth-century colonial poetry at its best."

Whose broad stripes and bright stars, through the perilous fight,

Ms. Parrish: "There's the old 'stars and stripes' merde again. I hate these bastards. And as for 'perilous fight,' what do you expect? It's the Poor Little Americans up against the Big Bad Brits — and don't forget, we Canadians burned the White House a few years earlier, in 1812."

Mr. Fulford: "I appreciate the consonance: the sound of 'b' in 'broad' and 'bright,' and the 's' in 'stripes' and 'stars.' And how impressive that Mr. Key reverses the old 'stars and stripes' to become 'stripes and stars,' a nice switch that makes our ears perk up. Note the fine choice of adjective — 'perilous' — to modify 'fight.' The lyricist is well aware that every battle is potentially a fatal one. And do be aware of how 'fight' echoes back to 'light' in the first line, creating an interesting ABCA rhyme."

O'er the ramparts we watched, were so gallantly streaming?

Ms. Parrish: "I never liked the dropping of the 'v' in 'O'er'; it's one more example of Yankee stinginess and cheapness. But then these *are* the folks who gave the world 99¢ hamburgers and Wal-Mart. As for 'ramparts,' well, that was the only American magazine I ever read; it was spot-on in most issues, as I recall."

Mr. Fulford: "I've always loved the way the writer brings together two thoughts so daringly: they are watching 'O'er the ramparts' something that is 'gallantly streaming,' and it is, of course, the great 'stars and stripes' of the American flag. Quite moving, really."

And the rockets red glare, the bombs bursting in air,

Ms. Parrish: "'Rockets.' 'Bombs.' Need I say more? And they're not just going up in the air; they're 'bursting.' Let's have some good old Yankee-caused bloodshed, yes?"

Mr. Fulford: "Nice rhyme with 'glare' and 'air'; good sense of visual imagery with the redness of the rockets 'bursting.' It's like a painting in words."

Gave proof through the night,
That our flag was still there,

Ms. Parrish: "'Proof.' What a laugh. Remember Colin Powell trying to link Osama bin Laden with Saddam Hussein back in 2002 and 2003? Sure, sure: *there's* 'proof' for you! And as for the flag being 'still there,' what do you expect? And if it weren't, they'd lie about it anyway. This is chauvinism of the worst kind, from the most abominable type of nationalistic maniacs, our so-called Good Neighbours to the South. **Ha**."

Mr. Fulford: "Note how 'night' links us brilliantly back to 'light' in the first line and 'fight' in the fourth — good stuff. And that line, 'our flag was still there,' never fails to move me to tears. The Canadians once had a flag too with a meaningful symbol on it — that of the Union Jack of the Mother Country. Now a stupid maple leaf. Only a bitter reminder that the Toronto hockey team hasn't won since the late 1960s."

> *Oh say, does that Star Spangled Banner yet wave,*
> *O'er the land of the free*
> *and the home of the brave.*

Ms. Parrish: "Gag me with a spoon. We even get a plug for the song itself with the title prominently echoed in the last lines, like a vulgar product placement in a Hollywood flick! And the 'Oh say' is far cruder than the simple beauty of 'O Canada.' As for 'the land of the free / and the home of the brave,' gimme a break. Ask the genocidal victims of the Indian Wars if that land is so 'free.' Typical Yankee vanity and blindness."

Mr. Fulford: "A perfect ending to a near-perfect national anthem. The poet even looks to the future with his powerful question about whether the American flag still does 'wave,' which I admire. And the rhyming of 'wave' and 'brave' in the third last and last lines is a fine touch. I never fail to be moved by the ending of this patriotic *cri de coeur*. A great anthem of a great nation."

> *On the shore dimly seen throughout the mists of the deep*
> *Where the foe's haughty host in dread silence reposes*
> *What is that which the breeze o'er the towering steep*
> *As it fitfully blows, half conceals, half discloses?*
> *Now it catches the gleam of the morning's first beam*
> *In full glory reflected now shines on the stream.*
> *'Tis the Star-Spangled Banner, Oh long may it wave*
> *O'er the land of the free and the home of the brave.*

Ms. Parrish: "Oh, Jeez, there's *more?* I hate these bastards. Look, I've got to go to the washroom. Talk to my assistant if you want any more insights into this so-called poetry. Something isn't poetry just because it rhymes, you know."

Mr. Fulford: "Look, I've got a column for the *Post* to finish up. But it's a shame that the later stanzas are never sung. I think there are two more as well; it would be good to hear them all, which might let Americans and Canadians learn some patience before the athletic contests finally start."

A SCHOLARLY STUDY OF THE CANADIAN NATIONAL ANTHEM

by Half a Dozen U.S. Talk-Show Hosts, Some University Professors of Canadian History and Culture, and a Number of American Scholars of Nineteenth-Century Poetry of the New World

O Canada! Our home and native land!

"An awful lot of exclamation marks for a rather unexciting country."

"Does 'native' refer to their Aboriginals? Didn't they slaughter most of them or put them on reservations?"

"If 'native' refers to being born in that tundra, then it really doesn't make much sense; Canada has more immigrants than 'natives,' to the best of my knowledge. Been in Hongouver or Torontopolous recently — *eh*?"

True patriot love in all thy sons command.

"Funny to see the word 'patriot' in anything written about Canada; what do *they* know about patriotism?"

"The 'sons' reference is unpleasantly sexist, but what does one expect from a nation of Eskimos and penguins?"

"'Command'? *Command whom*? When have the Canucks ever fought for anything except a puck? And that's the only thing on the ice that is black — ever noticed that?"

With glowing hearts we see thee rise

"'Glowing hearts'? Shouldn't that read 'glowing hearths'? Ever been in Winnipeg in February?"

"Nice to see 'hearts' and 'love' in a national anthem; sounds like a love poem. But what's to love on a godforsaken glacier?"

"'See thee rise' has a nice anachronism to it; you never hear 'thees' and 'thous' in poems much after Shakespeare.

But then the 'rise' could be a great plug for Viagra if it were around when this doggerel was written."

The True North strong and free!

"What a laugh. 'Strong and free'? *With what army?*"

"Well, it certainly is 'North'; I'll grant the hewers of water and drawers of wood *that* much."

"But 'free'? Ever try to get away buying something up there without being hit by a provincial tax *and* some kind of value-added tax they have?"

From far and wide, O Canada, we stand on guard
for thee.

"If 'far and wide' refers to the half a million immigrants they accept every few weeks, and most of them future terrorists from what I hear, then this lyricist was certainly prescient."

"'Stand on guard'? I'll say it again: *with what army?*"

God keep our land glorious and free!

"So much for the division of church and state. Those frozen buggers are doomed."

"It's about time we see 'God' in a national anthem; maybe the Canucks *aren't* godless communists like I've always heard about them; Cuba is overrun with the little icicle-ridden idiots."

"'Glorious'? Maybe the Rockies are, but what else? And 'free'? *With what army?*"

"'Free'? What a laugh. Ever see what they charge for gas up there?"

O Canada, we stand on guard for thee.
O Canada, we stand on guard for thee.

"Clearly, the so-called poet who penned this nonsense ran out of rhymes; maybe his pen froze."

"If they think that repeating 'stand on guard' three times in their national anthem will let listeners ignore the fact that they haven't spent 50¢ (Canadian!) on defence since the Korean War, they've got another thing coming."

"'Stand on guard?' What a laugh. *With what army?*"

"I'll take our 'Star Spangled Banner' any day of the week over their chicken-shit anthem, which makes no sense. At least our baby has some real patriotic feelings in it. But if those Canadian bitches Céline Dion and Shania Twain try to sing it again at one of our Super Bowls, I'll shoot them with my own gun and get away with justifiable homicide. EVER HEARD OF THE SECOND AMENDMENT?"

MONARCHISM VERSUS REPUBLICANISM:
OR,
THE GRASS IS ALWAYS GREENER

THE CANADIAN VIEW

Canada has always been a monarchy, all the way back to when the Natives were given Bibles, syphilis, and speeches on the king of England (or France) in welcome exchange for their land. And as recently as 1867 — "yesterday" in the mind of a Canadian monarchist — this young country reaffirmed its belief in the Crown.

Sadly, most Canadians, if asked who is the head of state of this country, would probably answer "The prime minister!" Or, almost as bad, "The governor general!" Actually, more Canadians would probably say "The president" and not be too far off the mark, especially after the Free Trade Agreement went through.

But the head of state of Canada is, in fact, Her Majesty the Queen. All Canadian laws are enacted in her name, proclamations issue from her, and MPs, cabinet ministers, civil servants, and the many dozens of members of the Canadian Armed Forces all take their oaths to her. The governor general, who, we charitably admit, opens a mean hospital and an exotic First Nations dance troupe now and then, merely performs duties on the queen's behalf.

I am sorry to report that recent polls have clearly shown that the vast majority of Canadians do not think that the royal family is "good for the country" or even good for each other, although that's a different matter. Whose fault is this? Probably that of recent federal governments in Ottawa, who have moved Canada inexorably, if not fatally, toward the American system of so-called republicanism. They wish to forget that one of the key facts differentiating us from the Americans is that Canada is a *constitutional monarchy*.

As the Monarchist League of Canada (3050 Yonge Street, Toronto, 416-482-4157; give it a call before you finish this chapter, please) never fails to point out, what has made this cold land so special is that our loyalty has always been to a person (the queen, of course; I hope you've been reading, not skimming, here) and not to some dangerous abstraction such as "country."

Unlike the United States, with its brutal racism and complex class system, Canada has always been One Happy Family, with the queen sitting regally at the head of the table, Philip doing the dishes in the kitchen, and our Aboriginals running the casinos out back. Canada has shown the world that the best way to express one's love of country is by showing loyalty to the Crown, not to a flag or an eagle or a movie star or by singing out at the top of your lungs "God Bless America" (written by a Russian-born Jew anyway. The guy also wrote "White Christmas" and "Easter Parade." Go figure).

Most potentially dangerous to the great tradition of the monarchy in Canada is the push to remove or downgrade

the sovereign through frequent attempts to update the
Citizenship Act, last tabled in the fall of 2002.

The present Citizenship Oath, created in 1977, goes like this:

I _____ *(LaBron/*
Igor/Moishe/Eufemia/Luigi/Abdul/Wang/Yigal/Pham/
Bishwa/etc.) swear (or affirm) that I will be faithful and
bear true allegiance to Her Majesty Queen Elizabeth the
Second, queen of Canada, her heirs and successors,
according to the law, and I will faithfully observe the laws
of Canada and fulfil my duties as a Canadian citizen.

Fine. It served us perfectly well for a quarter century, unlike
a recent waiter I had in an Edmonton restaurant. But what
many MPs in Ottawa have been pushing for is a revised
Citizenship Oath along the line of

From this day forward, I pledge my loyalty and allegiance to
Canada and Her Majesty Elizabeth the Second, queen of
Canada. I promise to respect our country's rights and free-
doms [author's note: this sentence is only going to turn
countless legal and tax-paying residents of this country,
who happen to be international terrorists on the side, into
liars, and as we well know *nobody* trusts a liar], *to uphold*
our democratic values [ditto], *to faithfully observe our laws*
and fulfil my duties and obligations as a Canadian citizen.

One can see the dilemma: gone is the "swearing" noted in the
1977 oath; gone is "faithful"; gone are "her heirs and successors" (when Charles's boys are *so cute*, clearly from Diana's
side). Even more dangerous is the Yankee-like insistence on

"democratic values" in the proposed new Citizenship Oath. This is the slippery slope of republicanism, even if it comes *without* loaded guns and crowded ghettoes.

This is why countless Canadians support the Monarchist League and are continually purchasing its many offerings of queen love, a few of which are listed here for your shopping convenience.

- A set of silver-plated spoons adorned with likenesses of the queen and Prince Philip: $14.95.
- A set of silver-plated spoons showing Prince Charles dating various porno queens: $39.95.
- The actual knife that Prince Philip shoved into the back of that divorced guy that Princess Margaret, rest in peace, foolishly considered marrying: $2,500.
- A postcard of the queen and Prince Philip in garter robes: 50¢.
- A postcard of the queen in nylons and garters in a failed attempt to satisfy Prince Philip: $1,800.
- A postcard of the queen at Balmoral with corgis: 75¢.
- A postcard of a pack of the queen's corgis attacking Pierre Trudeau: $25.
- An original oil painting of all the Nazi sisters- and brothers-in-law of Prince Philip, with a few of the queen's Nazi relatives milling about in the background: $10,000.
- A large postcard of Guy Burgess, Donald Maclean, and Kim Philby, all proudly singing "God Save the Queen": 90,000 rubles.

THE AMERICAN VIEW

The American government, unlike the Canadian, is not based on the monarchy but, indeed, was originally a reckless escape from it.

In truth, Americans pledge their allegiance to the flag every day in schools, almost hourly at home. "I pledge allegiance to the flag of the United States of America and to the republic for which it stands, one nation under God, indivisible, with liberty and justice for all." The "under God" part is a later addition and is being challenged in the courts as unconstitutional, but we can all hope that those words will stay. With God on their side, the Americans can pretty well do anything they want with, and to, the world.

Americans, then, do not believe in the monarchy since words and symbols such as "flag," "republic," "nation," and "Put your hands up; anything you say can be used against you; you have the right to a lawyer" mean everything to them, even if "liberty and justice" don't always refer to all U.S. citizens, especially since September 11.

But the dirty little truth that Americans refuse to confront (and a first tenet of good psychotherapy is that to deal with a problem you first have to recognize it) is that they suffer from monarchism envy. Look at the Rockefellers. The Roosevelts. The Fords. The Kennedys. The Clintons. The Bushes. Ted Turner and Jane Fonda. Ted and Tina Turner. All royal family substitutes. Just as telling is that litmus test of American popular belief, *People* magazine. In 2002 alone, either Princess Diana or her two sons by Prince Charles were on seventy-three covers. This was nearly half a decade after her death.

In spite of all their passionate denials, the American people long to have a king (Elvis?), a royal family (Kirk and Michael Douglas?), or a queen (Liberace?) to believe in, and they never really got over the American Revolution, obviously more of a teenage rebellion against mom and pop back in England. But they are too embarrassed to admit it.

Canada Continues to Invade the United States

In the great imperialist tradition of Toronto-born actress Mary Pickford becoming "America's Sweetheart" in the first quarter of the twentieth century, a Canadian-born woman named Jennifer Granholm, forty-three, was elected governor of Michigan in the fall of 2002.

The Harvard-educated former prosecutor and attorney general of the state, dragged against her will to California by her Canadian parents at the tender age of four, was, interestingly, attacked by her opponents more for her blonde good looks and western, non-Michigan background than for the fact that she had been born in a foreign country.

Also informative is the fact that Ms. Granholm never hesitated to discuss her "Canadian roots" during her bitter campaign. She told reporters during her run that she had been deeply influenced by her birth in Vancouver (she is still damp, presumably) and had been raised by parents who'd imbued her with "Canadian values." To add insult to injury, she continued, "I think the idea that Canada has a wonderful social safety net has always stuck with me. My parents have always said that it's a kinder, gentler nation." Yet she still won.

Because Governor Granholm was not born in the United States, all talk of her "making a good president" has been quelled — she would be legally unable to run for that high office. And Arnold, too.

This fact frees critics to suggest that what Ms. Granholm really said about Canada was that, compared with the United States, it is a "kinder, more *Gentile* nation."

BARBIE:
ICON OF WOMANHOOD,
MODEL FOR MILLIONS,
SLUT?

Could any toy be more symbolic of American womanhood than the Barbie doll? Yes, that sexy, pinched-waist, consumer-mad (the clothes, the van, the accessories) young woman who can play at fairy princess one moment and hard-working vet the next is still every girl's dream of her grown-up self. And let's face it, Canadian girls love Barbie too.

But as recently as February 2003, a Barbie controversy exposed some deep truths about how Canadians and Americans view sexuality, the female body, and just how much kids ought to know where they come from. It centred not on Barbie herself but on another doll in the Barbie line, her friend Midge. *"Has Ken Been Naughty?"* was the headline above an article about a Mattel doll available for purchase in both nations, with the subtitle "Pregnant Midge May Be Too Racy for Some Americans, but She's Flying out of Canadian Stores."

What happened was this: Mattel created a $30 pregnant doll, which led to "a storm of complaints in the United States" and forced Wal-Mart stores across that country to pull her off the shelves until she started menstruating again. To Americans, "pregnant Midge" suggested the "condoning of premarital sex by teenagers." That's what the vast majority of Yankee complaints insisted. In Canada, however, the same doll (which wears a wedding ring and is described on the packaging as being married) caused no protests.

Why such different responses? According to the Canadian manager of sales at Zeller's, who was thrilled to see Make-Out Midge flying off the shelves of his stores, "It's a different culture. In the U.S., they tend to be more inclined to censorship." When the Zeller's manager was told that Americans also yank music CDs with racy covers off their shelves far more often than Canadians do, he replied, "Canada is more of a liberal place than the U.S. We're more accepting." The Zeller's toy-man had a further thought: "In Canada, we're so multi-ethnic that we're more open-minded than people in the Bible Belt [where the head office of Wal-Mart is located, in Bentonville, Arkansas]."

Perhaps the problem was that many Americans automatically assumed that Barbie's best friend was still single like her virginal friend. Midge, however, is part of an entire "family line," which includes husband/father/sperm provider Alan, who comes with son Ryan in a stroller, sold separately. "It's kind of promoting kids to have kids," said a teenager who worked at an American Wal-Mart. And a mother of two (one wonders how she got them), strolling along an aisle at another store, was quoted as saying that she would never buy Midge the Whore for her first grader: "For me, I don't think Pregnant Midge is right for the kids. It's not like my daughter doesn't know what pregnancy is, but it's something a mother talks about. A Barbie can't talk about it."

Or perhaps it is the sheer horror that Americans feel when confronted with a toy implying that the act of sex has taken place, in or out of marriage. Canadians, it seems, have a more relaxed attitude about the subject. A young mother in Toronto, spotted shopping for her daughter's fifth-birthday present at a Wal-Mart, said, "My daughter is always pretending that she's a little mom and imitating me in every way, so we'll see how this goes over." She then tucked the box into the lap of her youngest child, a toddler (and, presumably, future fallen woman), in her stroller.

Karen Caviale, editor and publisher of *Barbie Bazaar*, a Wisconsin-based magazine that serves adult collectors of Barbie dolls, was upset with her fellow Americans. "In my opinion, it's making a mountain out of a molehill. They want to blame the decline of society on a doll. But a doll is totally innocent; it's what you project onto it that can make it seem offensive."

Oh, Midge. And we had so much respect for you. No more invitations to Barbie's pool parties for you.

And, hey, what's that grin on Ken's face for? You don't think. . . .

BUMPER STICKERS: POETRY IN MOTION

People may drive cars, but it's The Car that runs the economy. Just ask the workers on the line in Detroit, Michigan, or Windsor, Ontario. Maybe that's why cars have become such an expression of personality for both Americans and Canadians — from the make and colour, to the interior, to all the extras. And, of course, the bumper sticker.

Ah, the bumper sticker, otherwise known as the personal mobile billboard. Got an opinion? Want everyone to know that you love horses/sailing/bluegrass/Jesus/bondage? Well, some entrepreneurial kid with a few bucks and access to a print shop has printed just the slogan you want — sticky backing included in the price. And it shouldn't be surprising that Americans and Canadians express their inner selves through this haikulike form. Here are some Canadian and American bumper stickers, placed in pairs to illuminate their respective national psyches.

American (after 9/11/02): ONE THING THEY CAN NEVER DESTROY IS MY AMERICAN SPIRIT!
Canadian: FORGET ABOUT CBC. WHAT'S ON CABLE?

American: RED, WHITE, AND BLUE: MY COLORS DON T RUN!
Canadian: RED TORIES AND RED LIBERALS; IS THERE NO PLACE TO RUN?

American: NO GUTS, NO GLORY
Canadian: NO GUNS, NO TORIES

American: LET'S ROLL!
Canadian: SK8ER BOI

American: OUR FLAG MEANS EVERYTHING TO ME!
Canadian: OUR FLAG USED TO *MEAN* SOMETHING WHEN IT HAD THE UNION JACK

American: I VOTED IN THE 2000 ELECTION, AND ALL I GOT WAS THIS LOUSY PRESIDENT
Canadian: I'VE STOPPED VOTING BECAUSE IT REALLY DOESN'T MATTER ANYWAY, DOES IT?

American: SUPPORT OUR TROOPS!
Canadian: SUPPORT OUR TROOPS; HAVE A BAKE SALE

American: LIVE FREE OR DIE
Canadian: LIVE HEALTHY OR DIET

American: BUY AMERICAN!
Canadian: SELL TO THE AMERICANS!

American: BIN LADEN — DEAD OR ALIVE!
Canadian: JOE CLARK — IS HE DEAD OR ALIVE?

American: PROUD TO BE AMERICAN

Canadian: RELATIVELY HAPPY NOT BEING AMERICAN, I GUESS

American: THE STARS AND STRIPES FOREVER

Canadian: THE MAPLE LEAF — FOR NOW, ANYWAY

American: BOMB IRAQ!

Canadian: I GOT BOMBED LAST NIGHT; I'M A WRECK

American: LAND OF THE FREE, HOME OF THE BRAVE

Canadian: LAND OF THE FREEZE, HOME OF THE BLAHS

American: BOMB TORONTO

Canadian (Western): BOMB TORONTO

American: ONE NATION, UNDER GOD

Canadian: TWO NATIONS, UNDER SNOW

American: I AM SORRY TO HAVE BUT ONE LIFE TO GIVE TO MY COUNTRY

Canadian: I AM SORRY, BUT I HAVE ONLY ONE SIX-PACK LEFT

American: THE U.S.A. — NUMBER ONE, AND DON'T YOU FORGET IT!

Canadian: CANADA — WAY UP THERE WITH SOME OF THE BETTER COUNTRIES IN THE WORLD, SOME SAY

One of Canada's great newspaper moguls — at least until 2000 — was Conrad Black, who chose to give up his Canadian citizenship in order to move to the United Kingdom and become a lord.

Americans, no matter how powerful and wealthy, would never do such a thing since they already know that, without even leaving their country, each is a god.

PART 3:

Seats of Power

LET US COMPARE LEADERS

The true nature of a people is often revealed, for better or worse, by the leaders whom they elect or, in the case of George W. Bush in 2000, purportedly elect. Here are two comparative sets of statesmen, each expressive in his way of the country that he came to embody. The first two might be considered the real (if not historical) fathers of their nations: Abraham Lincoln, who saw the United States through a devastating civil war fought over the issue of race, and Pierre Trudeau, who nearly brought his country into a civil war over language and culture.

ABRAHAM LINCOLN, AMERICAN PRESIDENT

Lincoln was the son of a Kentucky frontiersman, which is like someone who lived on the Canadian prairies but enjoyed better weather. As the politician later sketched his life story, "I was born February 12, 1809, in Hardin County, Kentucky. My parents were both born in Virginia, of undistinguished families. My father had gone to Indiana, in my eighth year; a wild region, with many bears and other wild animals in the woods. [Why, this great man almost sounds like a Canadian.] There I grew up; somehow, I could read, write, and cipher, but that was all. [No, maybe not.]"

Lincoln worked hard at attaining knowledge, laboured on a farm, split rails for fences, and ran a store at New Salem, Illinois. He killed Indians in the Black Hawk War, spent eight years in the Illinois legislature, and served as a court lawyer for many years. In 1858, Lincoln ran against Stephen A. Douglas for senator of his state. He lost, but by debating with this man the future president gained a national reputation that won him the Republican nomination for president in 1860 without any oil money whatsoever.

The same year, Lincoln was elected the sixteenth president of the United States, building the Republican Party into a strong national organization. Interestingly, he had no religious affiliation, which would get him absolutely nowhere in the Republican Party of fourteen decades later. Most historians believe that Lincoln saved the United States by rallying Northern Democrats to the cause of the Union and by issuing an emancipation proclamation that freed the slaves within the confederacy.

Lincoln had a remarkable gift for words considering that he did not have David Frum around to help him. In his famous Gettysburg address at the military cemetery, he declared, "the dead shall not have died in vain, that this nation, under God, shall have a new birth of freedom, and that government of the people, by the people, and for the people, shall not perish from the earth." Of course, in the minds of most Americans, the term "people" did not refer to women and, for another century, most blacks either.

Lincoln won reelection in 1864 as the Union military were rapidly becoming *Gone with the Wind*. He showed a Canadian-like character by being flexible and generous as the horrific Civil War ground to an end, urging Southerners to lay down their arms, join the Union speedily, and, most important, vote Republican. On April 14, 1865, Lincoln was assassinated at Ford's Theater in Washington by a disgruntled actor from a famous family of performers who clearly was still recovering from terrible critical reviews.

PIERRE ELLIOTT TRUDEAU, CANADIAN PRIME MINISTER

Pierre Trudeau was the Abraham Lincoln of Canada in that, to quote Montreal poet Irving Layton, "he was the first Prime Minister of Canada worthy of assassination."

As prime minister from 1968 to 1984, with a brief cease-fire in 1979–80 (another interesting parallel with Lincoln), Trudeau gave the Canadian people what they wanted: TV in the House of Commons, less foreign ownership, a lower voting age, and more opportunities for youth. Indeed, he even married one.

Trudeau also gave Canadians what *he* wanted: recognition of both the Vatican and the People's Republic of China (a remarkable balancing act: the former wanting everyone to have a dozen kids; the latter insisting on only one). Also bilingualism, biculturalism, and bisexuality — the last one through reform of the Criminal Code. The National Energy Policy, which helped to alienate western Canada as much as the issue of slavery alienated the southern United States. Less access to utterly unnecessary government information. Banister slides. Queenly pirouettes. Movie-star girlfriends. And 465 irritating Québécois arrested and held without bail. (To be fair, these incarcerations were supported by the Canadian people, which says plenty about the rest of us.)

Described as "a priceless asset to the industrialized world" by the wildly successful American politician Walter Mondale, who probably meant that nobody could afford him, Trudeau became admired around the world simply by asking the important questions. "Where's Biafra?" (It was in Nigeria, but until the PM alerted voters who knew?) He also asked "Why should I sell your wheat?" — thereby suggesting that the government has no place in the farms — or the bedrooms — of the nation. And he was just as charming when he made a request. "Get off your asses; get out there and work" (said to protesters in Vancouver, who ignored their prime minister; unemployment remained high in British Columbia for many years after). Trudeau also told the truck drivers of Montreal to "mangez le merde," which thrilled the public, who wanted to tell off the posties as well. Plus this was the only French that they actually understood.

Over his remarkably long tenure in office, Trudeau received countless accolades. He was called "the magus" and "the alchemist." Of the latter there is no doubt; he managed to turn the Canadian dollar into shit.

Joseph Phillippe Pierre Yves Elliott Trudeau was born on October 18, 1919, in Montreal. His father opened a gas station in 1921 and sold it a little over a decade later for $1.4 million to Imperial Oil, teaching the young man the importance of one's inheritance. Mrs. Trudeau had a profound influence on her son until she passed away. He lost contact with her after that, unlike a previous Liberal prime minister with his mother (see below). Having grown up speaking French to his father and English to his mother, young Trudeau learned the importance of bilingualism, which he would eventually shove down the throats of his fellow Canadians. (Often an *accent aigu* or a circumflex would get lodged there, but with proper treatment most Canadians, especially westerners, were speaking only English again within a few weeks.) "Reason before passion" became his credo, and throughout his life he had no trouble reigning in any unhealthy passions for such unimportant subjects as economics, unemployment, Margaret, inflation, friends, and, of course, the Canadian west.

A valiant fighter during World War II — against conscription — Trudeau received an excellent grounding in learning while his fellow Canadians were carelessly getting shot to bits overseas: Harvard, the Sorbonne, the London School of Economics. Trudeau then hiked around the world, getting to know the planet before he could save it. He was in Vietnam just before the French were kicked out; in China just before the Communists took over; in Shanghai just before the city fell to the Reds. He would continue this pattern years later in public office.

Then, in 1965, in his mid-forties, Trudeau landed the first job he ever had: he was elected a Liberal MP. He had been a socialist up to that time, but since that group never seemed to get into power he chose to go with "les idiots." In 1967, Trudeau was a most innovative justice minister, modernizing a Criminal Code so outmoded that it was positively criminal. Everyone agreed with his profound insight that the state had no business in the bedrooms of the nation.

It was only when his wife made a business about the state of her bedroom that he felt things had gone too far.

In the election of 1968, Trudeau managed to bring sex out of the bedroom and into Canadian politics, where it had never before reared its ugly head or even derrière. Public hysteria, labelled "Trudeaumania" by psychiatrists, overwhelmed the nation. (Although it has lessened over the years, it appears, like herpes, to have no cure.) During the 1970 FLQ crisis, Trudeau managed to achieve something that had been done only to the country's citizens of Japanese origin a generation earlier: he took away the civil liberties of some twenty million Canadians. Always a man of honour, the prime minister invited his beloved people to just watch him, and they did.

For the next fifteen years, Prime Minister Trudeau worked continually to solve the unemployment problems of thousands of worthy Liberals by finding the poor souls jobs on government boards, royal commissions, countless agencies, and, of course, in the Senate. He also dated Barbra Streisand, Liona Boyd, and Margot Kidder, something that even Abraham Lincoln had never dreamed of.

During Trudeau's reign, unemployment across Canada did inch up just slightly, from 4.5% to 11.2%, and the inflation rate did rise somewhat, from 1.5% in late 1970 to 12.9%. True, the federal deficit nudged upward from $576 million in 1968 to around $30 billion when Trudeau left office in early 1984. But then, to be fair, Canada's inflation rate never reached the rate of Germany in the 1930s or Argentina in the 1980s. Trudeau just never had the time.

In October 2000, Pierre Elliott Trudeau finally died,

but he left his fellow citizens with an important lesson in Canadian politics: if you give them a finger, they take a Salmon Arm. He also taught every citizen of this great land that, when you are forced to work with nobodies, it's not easy to achieve perfection.

FRANKLIN DELANO ROOSEVELT, AMERICAN PRESIDENT

Born in 1882 in Hyde Park, New York, FDR (as he was warmly called by friends and mistresses alike) attended Harvard University and Columbia Law School. His fifth cousin was Theodore Roosevelt, who served as the Republican president of the United States when our hero was still a young man, and this inspired him to enter public service — but as a Democrat. In 1905, he married Eleanor Roosevelt, whom Pierre Trudeau would never have glanced at twice. FDR won election to the New York Senate five years later; unlike members of the Canadian Senate, he actually did things there. And he did something else that Trudeau never did — he worked his way up.

When he was thirty-nine, Roosevelt was struck by polio, but he fought to regain the use of his legs. By 1928, still on crutches, he was elected governor of New York. Just four years later, FDR was elected president of the United States, raising the hopes of tens of millions who had been thrown out of work by the Great Depression. In the first year of his presidency, there were thirteen million unemployed, and almost every bank was closed. This sort of occurrence took years of leadership for Trudeau to accomplish.

In his first hundred days, Roosevelt proposed, and Congress enacted, a sweeping program to bring recovery to

63

business and agriculture, relief to the unemployed, help to those in danger of losing their farms and homes. This was seen as communism by many who didn't realize that the wealthy Roosevelt was actually saving capitalism in an impressively sneaky way. By 1935, as the United States staggered toward some kind of recovery, many businessmen and bankers turned against what was called the New Deal. They were upset that FDR had taken their country off the gold standard and allowed "deficits in the budget," amazing in retrospect considering that no one has managed to achieve greater deficits than later Republicans such as Ronald Reagan and George W. Bush.

Still, President Roosevelt showed them. He brought in social security, much heavier taxes on the wealthy (George W. could hardly wait to reverse them), and a gigantic work relief program for the unemployed. Maybe the president *was* a commie, after all.

In 1936, FDR was reelected by a huge margin, at which point he pushed his luck a bit too far, trying to "stuff" the Supreme Court, which had been busy overturning several of his most important New Deal measures. While the president eventually lost that *kampf,* he began a revolution in constitutional law, which from then on made the federal government legally able to regulate the economy. Canada, of course, had been doing that for centuries, starting with wampum.

Roosevelt's military support for England in the early years of World War II brought his country out of the Depression more than anything else. Of course, Canada's troops had actually begun fighting — and dying — in September 1939, a fact that Americans (especially in

Hollywood) prefer to overlook. With the attack on Pearl Harbor in early December 1941, President Roosevelt declared war on the Axis powers, and, as we all know from those movies, the Americans won it single-handedly for the good guys. Alas, as World War II was coming to an end (actually, it never ends; watch the History Channel on cable any night of the week), Franklin Delano Roosevelt's health collapsed, and FDR died on April 12, 1945, in Georgia, mistress by his side. Fortunately, he had previously managed to give away half of Eastern Europe to the warm embrace of Stalin.

WILLIAM LYON MACKENZIE KING, CANADIAN PRIME MINISTER

Over half a century after his timely death, Canadians still wonder whether their longest-serving prime minister was a true Canadian institution or merely belonged in one.

Certainly, Mackenzie King came by his leadership capabilities honestly, unlike most things that he did in his life. His grandfather was also an important politician: he became the mayor of Toronto at a time when a small three-storey, four-bedrooms-no-bathroom house could be purchased for less than $500. His claim to fame is that he led a minor revolt in 1837.

The most important person in Mackenzie King's life was his mother, Isabel Grace Mackenzie. She would have made an ideal wife for William, but unfortunately she was already married to his father, John King, with whom she moved to Berlin, Ontario, before the town changed its name owing to some skirmish overseas in the midteens of the new century.

Isabel Grace regaled her son with stories of her famous father's life, and young William vowed to uphold the honour of the family name. And eventually he did, over the dead bodies of thousands of Europeans whom he prevented from coming to Canada in the 1930s and 1940s.

As a teenager, the brilliant lad entered the University of Toronto, where he was nicknamed Rex, probably due to his hang-dog features. He led the normal life of a typical young student of the 1890s: studying, attending classes, and saving ruined women from the depths of depravity by making use of their services. He enjoyed the last the most.

While continuing his studies in England, the young King was offered a position in the administration of Wilfrid Laurier, who clearly needed the services of an English-speaking whoremonger. It wasn't easy for the young Canadian to tear himself away from the women of the streets of London, but duty — and mother — called. Indeed, in 1901, King wrote in his diary that he had told his mother at this time, "If I ever do become Prime Minister, or come near to such a mark, it will be due to your life and love that I have done so." His father briefly considered suing young William for alienation of affection but decided against it.

For the next seven years, King willingly worked long hours in Ottawa since there was nothing to do at night back then in that town either. Our government was different in those early years: Laurier was busy saving the country, not selling it. Even as a young man, King showed the moral leadership that would characterize his entire life: he negotiated an agreement with the imperial Japanese government that severely limited the immigration of Japanese to Canada. He also managed to stop immigration from India.

At thirty-three, King was elected to Parliament, serving as the minister of labour. Laurier went down to defeat in 1911, taking WLMK along with him, but by 1914 the bad penny had bounced back: King became head of the Rockefeller Foundation's new Department of Industrial Relations. This was even better than being buddies with Laurier: Rockefeller was a Yankee and had big bucks. By the end of the Great War, poor King had lost his father, his sister, his brother, and his mother. Fortunately, he'd managed to keep in touch with the last, who'd always been a fabulous correspondent.

Laurier died in 1919, and King was chosen leader of the federal Liberal Party. As always, King knew exactly what to do in the 1921 election: absolutely nothing. He realized, like a true federal Liberal, that, if he never outlined a clear and intelligible policy in his election campaign, he would irritate nobody. This brilliant concept of nonleadership has worked wondrously well for the federal Grits ever since, especially for Trudeau in 1980 when he ran against that famous Canadian rock group The Who.

On December 29, 1921, the grandson of the rebel took office as prime minister of Canada without a single shot being fired. Since his was a narrow majority, King boldly continued his policy, giving the Canadian people nothing. When he went to the people again in October 1925, the Tories had absolutely nothing to attack. This time the strategy didn't work, and King even lost his own seat, which made it tough for him to get the speaker's attention during Question Period.

But King soon recovered his parliamentary majority and defeated the Tories while destroying his hated enemy, Tory leader Arthur Meighen. King was big on hated enemies. In the 1926 campaign, King was helped greatly by his mother, who'd been dead for only a few years and thus was still strong enough to vote as often as possible, a revered Grit tradition. He won an easy majority and made lots of private little in-jokes with his deceased mom as he watched Richard Bennett replace Arthur Meighen, just in time for the Great Depression, when King would wisely be out of power. That's another revered Grit tradition.

Some people made fun of King because he was a bachelor in his fifties, but they never really understood what a rich and vibrant private life he had with his dogs and his mother. All of them would converse long into each night; indeed, many of the best ideas of the federal Liberal Party came from dead parents and deceased pets during those many years of King rule.

Alas, King never did find a woman who was right for him. She would have had to possess some specific qualities: born in 1843, the daughter of a great Canadian politician and rebel leader, and named Isabel Grace. As you can imagine, these requirements limited his dating options greatly.

As luck would have it, the Canadian people actually elected a Conservative government in the summer of 1930, freeing King from having to be responsible to his fellow citizens during those difficult economic times. As an old Canadian saying goes, "When the going gets tough, the

Grits get out." Still, the depths of the Great Depression found the Once and Future King in considerable happiness, even though out of power. He spoke to his mother regularly, which was fine; she answered, which was weird; he heard her answer and answered back, which was loony tunes.

In 1935, King chose the perfect slogan: King or Chaos. It had a nice ring to it, especially since most Canadians had no idea what it meant. But it's hard to argue with a great idea, especially when it comes from the deceased.

And so the late 1930s was a wonderful time for King, who celebrated the centenary of his grandfather's rebellion in 1937 and visited the Third Reich, where he became good buddies with another demagogue who was great with the dead. The leader of Canada found *Der Fuehrer* to be "charming" and thought that they had much in common. Both had lived in Berlin and had absolute power, and King wasn't too hot for Jews either. The only awkward moment came when the prime minister of Canada upset his host by stating that he had "no intention whatsoever" of taking any of Hitler's Jews off his hands. Still, it was a nice meeting of minds. King appreciated the way that Hitler had almost single-handedly eliminated unemployment in Germany by simply throwing Jews, communists, and homosexuals out of work. King thought that it was a super idea for Canada, but he regretted that there just weren't enough of each back home to make it work.

By 1940, while King's old chum Adolf was busy conquering the other side of the Atlantic, King had been reelected with another overwhelming majority. Once again the PM found himself with nothing to do and endless time on his hands, so he was often free to call his mom long distance and charge it to the Canadian Treasury. He just sat back, let 'em be slaughtered over in Europe, hired C.D. Howe as minister of everything, kibbitzed with Mom, played and talked with his dogs Pat I, Pat II, and Pat III, and let the clouds of war roll by.

In 1948, King surpassed Sir Robert Walpole's record of leadership: 7,619 memorable days in office. At last, King decided that it was time to step down. But was it the right moment? Like any twentieth-century intellectual, the philosophical King checked the alignment of the stars to determine the best date. To this very day, astrology has been important to the federal Liberal Party; how else could it have chosen giants such as John Turner?

In sum, William Lyon Mackenzie King performed masterfully. He kept Canada united throughout the war, made the Liberals the true ruling party of the country, used the War Measures Act to incarcerate thousands of Japanese Canadians, and kept out as much Central and Eastern European riffraff as possible. Somewhere, as you are reading these words, King is frolicking with Pat I, Pat II, Pat III, dozens of fallen women whom he often "bent over" (to quote Mordecai Richler), as well as the purest woman that this country has ever known: Isabel Grace Mackenzie King.

It has been noted that Canada, unlike the United States, has more oil reserves than Saudi Arabia.

It has also been pointed out that the United States is more democratic than Canada in that its ruling party will be replaced sooner or later.

THE SENATE

UNITED STATES

The framers of the American Constitution created the U.S. Senate "to protect the rights of individual states and safeguard minority opinion in a system of government designed to give greater power to the national government," eventually located in Washington, DC. (Washington, by the way, is a pretty dangerous place these days, where you might be stabbed and left for dead. In Ottawa, your worst fears are to be bored and frozen to death.)

The creators of the Senate wanted it to be an independent body of responsible citizens who would share power with the president and the House of Representatives. To balance power between the large states and the small ones, the makers of the Constitution agreed that all states would be represented equally in the Senate, so that a state with fewer than half a million inhabitants would have the same number of elected senators — two — as a state with tens of millions of citizens. The idea that one man or woman (well, OK, man) from, say, Wyoming, has the same amount of power and importance as a man (yep) from California, which has over sixty times the population, isn't exactly democratic, but it does help to prevent what that nineteenth-century French fellow Alexis de Tocqueville called the tyranny of the majority.

To this day, the U.S. Senate, with its one hundred members, each elected for six years (unless voted out for moral or financial turpitude), is called "the most exclusive club in the world," which goes to show how little the pundits know about the cliques that I struggled to get into back in high school.

CANADA

Unlike the U.S. Senate, the Canadian Senate is considered the "Upper House" of our Parliament, which presumably means that its members are above the lowly goings-on of the other one. Unlike many of the weirdos elected to the Senate to the south, every one of its members is a winner. And the prize that each has captured is affectionately known as "Cash for Life." In fact, appointments to the Canadian Senate are no longer for life, for when a senator reaches the age of seventy-five the bucks tragically stop pouring in. But there's no need to organize a fund-raising concert with Bryan Adams; the pension remains generous.

Traditionally, there have been 104 members in the Canadian Senate, more than in the far more populous United States. Take pride in job creation, Canada. And many of them are still breathing: four from Prince Edward Island (a generous number that leaves hardly anyone left in that province to pick the potatoes); ten each from New Brunswick and Nova Scotia (since the Scots and Irish helped to build this land, not to mention thousands of great breweries); twenty-four from Quebec (many of whom speak French quite well); twenty-four from Ontario (many of whom speak English competently); six each from the four western provinces (where most would not speak French if you paid them and have enough trouble getting out a few words of English); one each from the Yukon and NWT (whenever they can catch the bush plane out); and six from Newfoundland (who are usually inarticulate in both official languages, not unlike our beloved prime minister of the past decade).

Recognizing the importance of these illustrious positions, the qualifications for getting into the Canadian Senate have always been extremely stringent. A candidate for senator has to be at least thirty years of age, a subject of the queen if not the object of her affection, own property worth at least $4,000 (which until recently was problematic for Newfoundlanders), and live in the area from which he or she is being appointed. Naturally, the most crucial qualification of all is to have been a fund-raiser (French *"sacmonsieur,"* English "bagman") for the federal party in power.

Detractors aside (and at most they number in the tens of millions), the Canadian Senate was given at least one important role: to provide "sober second thought" on legislation being discussed and passed by Members of Parliament, the men and women who are actually elected by their constituents. Sadly, the word *sober* is a foreign concept to many of the senators who are connoisseurs of the barley and the grape. It may come as a surprise to readers that the Canadian Senate actually possesses legal powers almost equal to those of the much-lower house. However, the Senate cannot raise money and has only a six-month veto on constitutional amendments — hardly enough time to get all the old guys back in the room again, let alone sober.

Like so many aspects of these two great countries, there are remarkably few differences between the U.S. Senate and the Canadian Senate. The U.S. Senate has many regularly meeting committees, such as Armed Services, Budget, and Foreign Relations. In other words, the deliberations and votes of the (elected) U.S. Senate have the fate of America, and much of the world, in their hands. Naturally, the Canadian Senate has its own numerous committee meetings, on everything from unemployment (a condition that the senators need not worry about personally until they reach seventy-five), poverty (never), and aging, a subject on which most of the senators are experts. Every attempt to reform or eliminate the Canadian Senate over the years has met with little success. But it would simply not be cost effective to destroy this great Canadian institution: does anyone realize what it would cost voters to build a new senior citizens' home in such a marvellous location?

Readers should not confuse the political Senate with the Ottawa Senators, an NHL team housed a few miles away. The differences between them are all too obvious. For example, the Ottawa Senators work together pretty well and have been known to actually achieve some goals. But they do have one essential trait in common with their political namesake: until recently, the Ottawa Senators could not raise money either.

There are many issues that Canadians and Americans disagree over, such as whether bombing is better than peace-keeping, when Thanksgiving should be celebrated, or whether stars and stripes are snazzier looking than a maple leaf. But there is one inarguable fact that will forever unite these two great countries in spite of their differences: *at forty degrees below, Celcius and Fahrenheit are the same*. Of course, Winnipeg knows this firsthand, often as late as May.

GREAT WORDS FROM GREAT STATESMEN

AMERICAN

The Congressional Record is the official account of the proceedings and debates of the U.S. Congress and is published daily when the houses of Congress are in session.

The elected federal members of the House of Representatives and the Senate are continually debating important topics of interest to their great republic and, when the discussions are about bombing foreign nations, to many other citizens around the world.

Here, verbatim, is a small portion of the transcription of a U.S. congressman's 1996 speech on the always entertaining subject of campaign finance reform.

Hon. John Lewis, a Representative in Congress from the State of Georgia:

Thank you for the opportunity to speak on this subject today.

The challenge and task that you are undertaking is formidable. Changing the way campaigns are financed is a difficult job, particularly because it is something that will dramatically impact all of our lives. But clearly something must be done. Too much time is spent raising money and the current system is one that has been criticized about the way our democracy works.

I commend you for holding these hearings and hope you can arrive at a formula which is fair, nonpartisan and nondiscriminatory and restores the American people's faith in our democracy. . . .

CANADIAN

Hansard is the record of parliamentary and legislative debates that take place in the Canadian House of Commons. Following are some typical exchanges from early February 2003, as recorded in Hansard, that suggest how the Canadian democratic process unleashes a torrent of brilliant and persuasive words, a testament to the idea that fair debate makes for a better society.

"Oh, shut up."

"*You* shut up."

"Hear, hear!"

"Where? Where? *Where??*"

"Mange le merde!"

"You appear to have strong opinions on that, Mr. Know-It-All. Well, I personally wish that your **mother** had believed as profoundly in abortion as you do."

"Order! Order!"

"Odour! Odour!"

"Nice dress, Elsie!"

"If the honourable member from Yellowknife had

even one single brain cell, it would die of loneliness."

"Oh, yeah? Now tell me, kind sir: which official language was *that* statement mumbled in?"

"You shouldn't have run for member of parliament, monsieur; you should have run for *cover*."

"Up yours!"

"Oh? *You* would probably enjoy that, Svend."

"To hell with prayers in Canadian schools. Why weren't *you* ever in a school?"

"Go suck on a lemon. It'll sweeten your disposition."

"Was that the French language which you were just trying to use, or did your dinghy just land on the coast of Nova Scotia?"

"Nice outfit! Was the guy still alive that you stole it from?"

"Why don't you stand up like an intelligent human being, or haven't you evolved to that level yet?"

"I *am* standing up, you heightist bastard!"

"Liar, liar, house on fire! Your nose is as long as a telephone wire!"

"Why don't you go back into the closet, where you belong?"

"Hey, numbskull, the camera just went off; you can go back to sleep now."

"Your argument for a $100 million new ocean port for your district is most admirable, honourable flacid member. But since you represent a riding in the Canadian prairies, I find it a bit excessive."

"Mr. Chairman, I resent that slur. I was born and raised in a communist dictatorship in Eastern Europe, where I was imprisoned and tortured endlessly, not unlike listening to that honourable idiot."

"Commie! Commie! Commie! Commie! Commie!"

"Oh, shut up. Just shut up, already. Just shut the fuck up!"

"I move that we adjourn for the afternoon. No — make that for the rest of the week."

PART 4

Our Men and Women in Uniform:
Or,
"Nice Forest Camouflage, Too Bad You're in the Desert"

OUR (POORLY) ARMED FORCES

Canadians have seen themselves primarily as "peace-keepers" since Prime Minister Lester B. Pearson won the Nobel prize for peace when he forced Britain, France, and Israel out of the Suez Canal (for which none of those countries — or Egypt, for that matter — ever forgave him). At that time, Canadian soldiers were sent in to keep the peace. And, looking at the peace that has existed in the Middle East ever since, our efforts have clearly worked.

But over the years, Canada has truly become "the penny stock" on the defence markets of the world. (It's a shame that the Vancouver Stock Exchange no longer exists.) Most Canadians would be surprised to hear that of 4,000 Canadian soldiers sent overseas in 2002 (which does not include Newfoundland, in spite of the half-hour time difference), only 230 wore blue berets, which are symbolic for *"Please don't shoot me. I'm a peacekeeper, here to keep the peace, or at least to try to find it."*

Those who think that Canada has lost its reputation as the world's peacekeeper should remember that, since hardly any bullets are provided for our soldiers, every member of our Armed Forces **is** a peacekeeper for all intents and purposes. Our boys and girls serve in the great Hollywood tradition of "Don't move, and nobody will get hurt!"

The state of our Armed Forces has descended to a truly extraordinary level of inadequacy, attracting the admiration of peaceniks around the world (many of whom live in northern British Columbia and toke weed all day). Here are some actual facts (I'm not making this up) regarding Canada's "nonfighting heroes," as they are sometimes called.

- Over fifty nations spend more per capita on defence than Canada does, including countries that have nationalized health care, boast far fewer citizens, and have substantially less land mass.
- Forty percent of Canadian fighting vehicles and weapons may be grounded by 2004 for lack of spare parts and technicians to fix them.
- Canada's Sea King helicopters are forty years old, nearly as old as the average Canadian soldier. In the spirit of bilingualism, I will translate the name: "Sea" as in "bottom of the"; "King" as in "King Lear." To be fair, these Sea King helicopters are "state of the art," the art being circa 1963.
- The United States has often turned to Canada in the past for "extra spear carriers" to help fight its battles, although it recently expressed disappointment on discovering that the Canadian Armed Forces were actually equipped with spears.
- A recent study by *Jane's Defense Weekly* reported that "there is more modern weaponry in the average U.S. high school than in the entire Canadian Armed Forces."
- A statement was released by the federal government in Ottawa in 2003 that Canada expects to assist in the rebuilding of Iraq in its own truly Canadian fashion — by accepting 8.5 million refugees from Iraq as new citizens.

- The 2002 U.S. budget for missile defence alone was $7.3 billion. The budget of Canada for defence against incoming missiles was $14.95, and that was only due to a great Internet deal that Ottawa got.

- A Gallup Poll in February 2003 noted that "60% of Canadians are willing to give up some personal freedom to fight terrorism in the world after 9/11, while 36% of the rest did not know that they had any."

- After four Canadian soldiers were killed by friendly fire in 2002 in Afghanistan, they were honoured with bronze stars from the U.S. government, which probably satisfied everyone involved and may have brought one or two of them back out of sheer pride.

- Canadian forces fighting in Kosovo and Afghanistan had to borrow bombs from the United States when they ran short. Being nice Canadians, they will no doubt return them in good condition.

- Canada is known and admired around the globe for having put "sub" back into "submarine." After all, so many of them go down without returning to the surface.

BOMBS AWAY

Here is a list of countries that the U.S. government has bombed since the end of World War II, bombing that failed to result in a democratic government or in greater respect for human rights.

China, 1945–46

Korea, 1950–53

China, 1950–53 (That's the trouble with Chinese food; just a few years later, you want to bomb again.)

Guatemala, 1954

Indonesia, 1958

Cuba, 1959–60

Guatemala, 1960 (Clearly, Guatemalan food has the same effect.)

Vietnam, 1961–73

Congo, 1964

Laos, 1964–73

Peru, 1965

Guatemala, 1967–69

Cambodia, 1969–70

El Salvador, 1980s

Nicaragua, 1980s

Grenada, 1983

Libya, 1986

Panama, 1989
Iraq, 1991–99; 2003–
Afghanistan, 1998
Sudan, 1998
Yugoslavia, 1999

And here is a list of countries to which the Canadian government has sent peacekeepers since the end of World War II, peacekeeping that failed to result in a democratic government or in greater respect for human rights.

See above.

Also add Cyprus, Egypt, Bosnia, Croatia, Rwanda, Somalia, et cetera.

But to be fair to our dozens upon dozens of armed warriors in the Canadian Armed Forces, who ever talks about Oka nowadays?

FRIENDLY FIRE

Canadian attitudes toward the United States were hurt by a "friendly fire" incident in April 2002 when four Canadian paratroopers were killed after two American pilots dropped a laser-guided, five-hundred-pound bomb on their live-fire exercise in Afghanistan, an exercise that the Yankees mistook for enemy fire.

Since these four young men were the first Canadian soldiers killed in a combat zone since the Korean War, the action irritated the families of the dead men. The media in the United States, naturally, saw the incident as minor and rarely followed the story, even though there were thrilling visuals from the F-16 warplane that dropped the bomb on the Canadians.

Some solace came to the families of the deceased when the two U.S. Air Force pilots were put on trial charged with involuntary manslaughter, with the Pentagon arguing that the men "disobeyed orders, lacked discipline, and exercised poor judgment." The lawyers for the two pilots countered with the fact that these three actions — disobeying orders, lacking discipline, and exercising poor judgement — are committed daily by their commander in chief, President George W. Bush, and no one puts *him* on trial.

In June 2003, the Air Force dropped criminal charges against the two fighter pilots and recommended instead "administrative discipline." This means for Major Schmidt the loss of a total of one month's pay, house arrest for thirty days, and confinement to a military base for sixty days, and Umbach could receive a letter of reprimand for failing as lead pilot to exercise "appropriate" control over Schmidt. Oh, and Umbach's recent request to retire from the Air Force might also be granted.

Meanwhile, the family of Private Richard Anthony Green of Hubbards, Nova Scotia, told the *New York Times* that the young Canadian soldier had a favourite saying that had always confused them: "Lord, protect us from our friends; our enemies we can handle."

This incident reminded Canadians that the United States is truly our nation's oldest and dearest friend, not to mention next-door neighbour. And Canadian citizens from coast to coast vowed, upon considering this friendly fire incident, that they had better not cross the United States but back it in its every endeavour in the United Nations, Iraq, and elsewhere, because, after all, we don't want to be *its* enemy.

Or is being its *friend* more dangerous?

PART 5

"Neither Hail, Nor Sleet, Nor Snow . . .": Or,

How the Countries Run

FLYING THE FRIENDLY SKIES

AIRLINES IN THE UNITED STATES

Nearly every major airline in the United States has either declared bankruptcy (United, USAir) or is teetering on the edge (American Airlines, Northwest, etc.). This from the country that taught the world how to fly and often to drop giant bombs while doing it.

AIRLINES IN CANADA

Canada has an impressive history of air travel, if only because the federal government has traditionally thrown billions of subsidy dollars at its national airline, Air Canada.

No other national airline in the world can fly passengers smokeless from Toronto to Ottawa and luggageless from Halifax to Port Arthur. (Most pilots, apparently, have not yet heard of the name change to Thunder Bay.)

Air Canada was first created in 1937 as Trans-Canada Airlines, but it came in the wake of a long history of aviation in Canada. In 1907, Alexander Graham Bell flew in a heavier-than-air kite (when he wasn't making nuisance phone calls), and two years later John McCurdy flew the *Silver Dart* under its own power. By 1930, a lighter-than-air dirigible reached Montreal from England. Unlike today, every one of those machines departed and arrived on time.

For over sixty-five years, Air Canada has been leading the way in this country's aviation business, especially because its endless government grants and decades-old Crown corporation status have allowed it to drive Canadian Airlines, Wardair, and other presumptuously for-profit companies into the ground. But then no one ever said that life, or air travel, was fair. That Air Canada begged for bankruptcy protection in April 2003 was typical, another sly plea for more of your tax dollars.

Just remember to bring your own sandwich.

Sure, airlines in the United States are in trouble too. But Canadians are always more willing to let their federal government bail out its businesses. One thing is for certain and in our country's favour: Air Canada should be admired for its status as world leader in what is called "bad-weather flying" since it operates four-fifths of all its flights in the worst weather conditions on Earth. And those are just the ones into and out of Vancouver.

DELIVER DA LETTER,
DA SOONER DA BETTER

THE U.S. POSTAL SERVICE

The Continental Congress named Benjamin Franklin the first postmaster general in 1775, even before the nation was founded. Since then, the U.S. Postal Service has helped to bind the nation together, almost as much as did crushing the Indians and promoting slavery.

Highlights in the history of the U.S. Postal Service include the first Dead Letter Office (1825), the use of postage stamps (1847), registered mail (1855), street letter boxes (1858), Pony Express (1860), free city delivery (1863), railroad post offices (1864), the penny postcard (1873), special delivery (1885), rural free delivery (1902), parcel post (1913), airmail (1918), ZIP codes (1963), and, most tragically, the end of subsidies from the federal government (1983), after which the service began to lose billions annually. In this last highlight, the Americans appear to have been inspired by Canada.

CANADA POST

With a population one-tenth that of the United States spread over an enormous expanse, Canada has been postally challenged from the start. Not until 1981 did the postal service in Canada become a Crown corporation. Its goal was to "break even within five years," but all it managed to do was fail to break its unions in six.

In 1797, when the tiny town of York (later the smug town of Toronto) was the capital of Upper Canada, letters reached its four hundred inhabitants once every winter by coach from Montreal. During the brief few weeks of spring and summer in Canada, mail came far more regularly — once a month.

As late as the 1870s — from which decade nearly all the mail sent has been delivered by now — postpersons would actually charge up to two pennies for the luxury of receiving letters! Today Canada Post continues this venerable tradition in its own special way by not giving two cents as to whether or not the mail gets to where it's addressed.

Other traditions survive. In 1875, the postmaster general of Canada ordered that "any piece of mail without adhesive stamps would be sent directly to the Dead Letter Office." Today merely the lack of a postal code will do the same — and far faster.

In this new millennium, Canada Post is a proud, multi-billion-dollar corporation that every day moves tens of millions of pieces of mail (among the many, many more posted). Unlike the U.S. Postal Service, which is harsh and cold, Canada Post has the sweetness and empathy that one would expect from an institution in our more caring, collective nation. Millions of emotionally hurtful "Dear John" and "Dear Mary" letters have never reached their destinations thanks to the human decency of Canada Post.

Unlike the harsh, right-wing, anti-union nature of the United States, Canada Post workers thrive in our union-loving clime. They have been known to attach witty stickers to envelopes: "STAMP OUT PRIVATIZATION" is one favourite; "STOP CONTRACTING OUT" is a touching *cri de coeur* against the loss of much-needed postal jobs. Even more common are the touching "WHAT AM I DOING HERE?" and "WHEN'S LUNCH?" and the always-good-for-a-laugh "RETURN TO SENDER."

Of course, e-mail now makes all of this redundant. As for packages, we have a respected, quality U.S. company to turn to. *Loved* the Tom Hanks movie.

I did have some last thoughts on comparing the postal services of both nations, but unfortunately I posted them to ECW Press, and they were lost in the mail.

ON THE AIR

PUBLIC RADIO IN THE UNITED STATES

NPR — National Public Radio — was created only recently, in 1967, when the U.S. Congress passed the Public Broadcasting Act. Its goal: to encourage "the growth and development of noncommercial radio" and to develop "programming that will be responsive to the interests of the people."

By early 1970, ninety public radio stations made up its charter members. And today, barely over a third of a century later, NPR serves nearly twenty million listeners a week via more than 680 member stations. (Unfortunately, that's actually the same hundred thousand people who just keep tuning in several times each day; the Americans clearly use the same counting method as Canada does with the CBC.) For those listeners, though, NPR is oral gold. To most in the U.S. Congress, it is aural communism.

THE CANADIAN BROADCASTING CORPORATION

Public broadcasting in Canada predates the American version by several decades. It was on November 2, 1936, when a Crown corporation was established, and the Canadian Broadcasting Corporation came to life. Actually, it was only *created* then; *coming to life* has taken considerably longer and is still a matter of debate, which is why "the Corp" is just as often called "the Corpse."

Early CBC highlights include

- the speech from the throne in both English and French in 1937;
- farm broadcasts in French in 1938;
- six weeks of nonstop coverage of the visit by King George VI and
- Queen Elizabeth in 1939 as well as the first farm broadcasts in English (you *had* to be there);
- the opening of the Alaska Highway — live! — in 1942 (you *didn' t* have to be there);
- the first fishermen's broadcasts in the Maritimes in 1946 (you didn't *want* to be there); and
- endless coverage of Princess Elizabeth and the Duke of Edinburgh's four-week royal tour in 1951 (*they* didn't want to be *here*).

Thanks to our revered socialist, let-the-feds-take-care-of-everything attitude, this tradition of noncommercial broadcasting came to television with the creation of CBC TV in 1952, beginning with CBFT in Montreal, then CBLT in Toronto. Most important, of course, was the birth of CKSO TV in Sudbury, Ontario, a year later, since those poor suckers lived so far north that they couldn't pick up the American shows and were really stuck.

The excitement of public broadcasting, when it finally came to the visual medium, was almost unbearable: *Uncle Chichimus. The Big Revue. Country Hoedown.* And best of all, before and after CBC TV went on the air each day, there were those intriguing test patterns.

Within a year, every Canadian within a hundred miles of the U.S. border and a tall-enough antenna was able to get what he or she **really** wanted: *Paul Whiteman's Teen Club. Beat the Clock. The Jackie Gleason Show. My Favorite Husband. Your Show of Shows. Your Hit Parade. You Asked for It. Walter Winchell. Quiz Kids. The Jack Benny Show. Toast of the Town. What's My Line. Roy Rogers. The Colgate Comedy Hour. The Perry Como Show. George Burns and Gracie Allen Show. Arthur Godfrey's Talent Scouts. I Love Lucy. The Red Buttons Show. Arthur Murray Dance Party. Name That Tune. Make Room for Daddy. Dinah Shore. Milton Berle Show. Fireside Theater. I've Got a Secret.* (My mom thought that one referred to the Gouzenko Affair, which was so Canadian that we didn't watch it for the first few years, darn it.) *I Married Joan. My Little Margie. This Is Your Life. The Lone Ranger. You Bet Your Life. Dragnet.* (We hear it's back in 2003 in a new version. Can't wait to catch it.) *The Adventures of Ozzie and Harriet. Mama. Topper. Our Miss Brooks. The Life of Riley.* And hundreds more.

It was a thrilling time, those first years of CBC TV, and it's a wonder that Canadians could get any work done at all. Especially with the CBC buying up American shows whenever possible and presenting them to more Canadians than ever before. After all, the great R.B. Bennett, back when the Corp/Corpse was created in the 1930s, had promised "equal enjoyment of the benefits and pleasures" of broadcasting; he hardly mentioned Canadian content, did he? And today, thanks to two major commercial networks (although the CBC has just as many commercials these days), CTV and

Global, our fellow citizens from sea to sea to sea can get all the American shows they want. God, but I love this country.

When television came to both the United States and Canada, it caused no less than a cultural revolution. Traffic stopped. Toilet pressure dropped in apartment buildings everywhere during commercial breaks. In the United States, everyone was home watching Uncle Miltie. In Canada, when Percy Saltzman tossed his chalk in the air, millions of our citizens held their collective breath until he caught it. Clearly, it didn't take much to entertain our citizens back in those days.

But it was that kind of era. Uncle Louis was in power in Canada, Dwight Eisenhower was at the helm in the United States, and rock 'n' roll wasn't available from white performers yet. Those years were the perfect time for television to hit the airwaves in both countries; there just wasn't anything else happening.

As for television today, viewers in both countries can raise their unified voices in one cry of gratitude: **"Thank God for cable."**

THE ROMANCE OF RAIL TRAVEL

AMERICA'S AMTRAK

The result of the merger of three American railroads, Amtrak officially began its service on May 1, 1971, leaving New York's Penn Station at 12:05 a.m. bound for Philadelphia. It arrived several weeks later — not an auspicious debut. But the corporation had only two dozen employees at its birth; today it employs over twenty-four thousand people, of whom over half actually work.

That first year, Amtrak announced a schedule of 184 trains serving 314 destinations. Just over three decades later, it now serves over five hundred stations in forty-six states. The only ones who miss out on the excitement and anticipation of whether or not their citizens will die, compliments of Amtrak, are Alaska, Hawaii, South Dakota, and Wyoming, a fact that stuns millions of Americans who always thought that the latter two are part of the contiguous states of the union. No doubt the citizens of these states resent missing out on Amtrak's regular crashes. After all, everybody likes a good train wreck now and then.

CANADA'S VIA RAIL

Via Rail Canada came into being as a subsidiary of

Canadian National Railways in 1977 and has been receiving subsidies ever since. With Via Rail, Canada has one of its few institutions that actually comes close to matching the success and respect of the one created for similar purposes in the United States: Amtrak. Indeed, Canada's Via Rail is widely admired from coast to coast and even in fields outside transportation. For instance, its "System Time-table" won the Governor General's Literary Award for Fiction in 1998. It is also famous for having encouraged the Canadian hero Rick Hanson, who would often zoom past a halted Via Rail train, inspiring him to complete his fund-raising wheelchair run across the country.

Canada's train system owns over one hundred diesel locomotives, some six hundred passenger cars, seventy-six self-propelled rail diesel cars, over fifty steam generators, dozens of "Light, Rapid, and Comfortable" (that's a euphemism) locomotives, and some one hundred LRC coaches, of which well over one-third work. Via officials often note that a .333 batting average in professional baseball would garner many awards and a high salary.

A major argument on behalf of Via Rail is the simple fact that, in terms of energy efficiency, the train (based on seat miles per gallon of fuel consumed) is twice as efficient as the bus, seven times more efficient than the automobile, and fourteen times as efficient as the airplane. The minor flaw in this logic is that, in each of those other modes of transportation, a person eventually reaches his or her destination.

There are, however, more valid defences of Via Rail. For instance, the corporation has been in the national forefront of focusing considerable public attention on the serious travel-related problems of the disabled. After all, Via's trains have difficulty getting around as well. And it is worth remembering that train service has improved radically over the past century. Back in 1892, Canada's transcontinental train averaged sixty kilometres an hour, which necessarily included frequent stops for coal and water. Today, over eleven decades later, the "transcon" averages sixty-one kilometres an hour, without all of those now needless coal and water stops. No, the stops today are for traction motor failure and countless other problems that neither you nor I nor Via's thousands of repairmen could possibly understand.

Despite its heartless critics, Via Rail is a precious part of Canada's heritage — much like our country's snow and cows, both of which have stopped many a train every week, often for half a day or more. It seems only fitting to quote the words of that great Canadian folk singer Gordon Lightfoot: "There was a time in this fair land when the railroad did not run."

These words are still true today.

SOME THOUGHTS ON THE TRAIN SERVICE OF EACH COUNTRY

Canadians love to feel superior and condescend to their wealthier and more numerous neighbours to the south; it is one of our greatest moral flaws, as the *National Post*'s Robert Fulford and American talk-show host and former presidential candidate Pat Buchanan have often pointed out.

Which is why I shall here favourably compare the powerful arguments on behalf of both Amtrak and Via Rail and their respective nation's financial support for each.

- Train passengers rarely fall from tens of thousands of feet in the air to certain death.

- Train passengers rarely lose their luggage, and even when they do it is never halfway around the world but in some friendly, English — or French-speaking (Canadian) or English- or Spanish-speaking (American) city and always returns within a few days. Or so.

- Treats are offered to first-class passengers of both Amtrak and Via Rail: complimentary cocktails (since, when you're drunk, you tend to lose track of time); full-course hot meals served right at your seat (since, when passengers mill about in circles around the train until it starts moving again, it can upset the conductor — and American conductors usually have loaded weapons); complimentary magazines and newspapers (and, thanks to the frequent breakdowns, chances to catch up on your reading); and even rotating seats (so you can look forward, to where you should have been heading, and backward, to where you should have left already).

- In Canada especially, all those "unscheduled stops," as Via officials subtly call them, are great opportunities for our citizens to marvel that the farmers who own all that fertile land somehow cannot make ends meet.

- Both the American and the Canadian train systems have taught their respective passengers that time really isn't so important in the Great Scheme of Things. An obsession with being on time is usually highly stressful, and we all know that stress is one of the greatest killers in the world today. Along with U.S. foreign policy, of course.

TAKING A NATION'S MEASURE

One of the most striking differences between our two great nations is the metric system, a fairly recent Canadian institution, even if it is still not entirely accepted by most Canadians, many of whom remain closet imperialists. (That's a pun, son.)

Most Canadians will be surprised to learn that the metric system was legal in this country as early as 1871. But then so was wife beating and electing drunks to the highest office in the land, and nobody complained about *those* problems. But while metric was legal in Canada for over a century before it became official, it was rarely used since most of our citizens would rather give an inch than take a metre. As in so many important aspects of Canadian life, citizens continued to follow the British system, based on yards, pounds, gallons, and other such unscientific concepts, which made perfect sense to everyone except the exasperated engineers and scientists who actually had to use measurements in their work.

American stubbornness in refusing to join every other nation on the face of the Earth in the twenty-first century in the use of the metric system — except for Burma and Liberia, the two other World Leaders in Reactionary

Measurement — reflects the rugged individuality and rejection of conformity that one expects from "The Greatest Country in the World." (This quotation was found in over a thousand letters to the editor in hundreds of American newspapers during the week of March 2–9, 2003.) Besides, America would face its own particular conversion problems. For example, what would Americans have called the Colt 44?

But in the 1960s, Mother England, to whom many hundreds of our citizens continue to look with reverence, awe, and admiration, went metric. Canada produced a white paper on metric conversion (which, shockingly, actually measured 8.5" by 11") setting out many recommendations for government policy on this vital topic.

The Metric Commission of Canada was appointed and soon gained the affectionate title of "The Kilometre Kops," a knowing nod to Quebec-born comedy director Mack Sennett, whose "Keystone Kops" were among the greatest creations of the silent-screen era. Then the Weights and Measures Act was passed by Parliament, and a new Consumer Packaging and Labelling Act required metric units to be shown on most consumer product labels, infuriating American branch-plant producers of products everywhere across Canada. Metric conversion was launched as a many-phased, many-splendoured program since the wise elected federal officials of Canada recognized that litres and metres were very good for its citizens, sort of like spinach.

Implementation in the United States would have been nearly impossible considering that the country is cruelly fragmented between blacks and whites, Spanish and

English speakers, the Union and the Confederate states, the rich and the poor, the Kennedys and everybody else. Not so Canada! No, within weeks a remarkable unification of the entire citizenry occurred in spite of our sparse population spread out across ten provinces and (at the time) two territories in the second-largest nation on Earth. There arose a solid, universally held hatred for the new metric system. This anger over metric united Canadians even more than their profound, justifiable dislike of Toronto.

The newspapers of Canada in the 1970s soon told the story: three of every four letters to the editor raged against "this commie plot of metrification." What millions of Americans felt about the removal of prayer in public schools was only marginally more passionate than Canadian feelings about losing our beloved inches and pounds. Ironic, considering our national obsession with dieting. The arguments reflected Canadian thought and philosophy at their finest. Here are a few opinions of the time, quoted from the *Ottawa Citizen*.

> *This idiotic move to bring metric to Canada is simply too much. Next, they'll start letting in every immigrant in the world. A woman who poses for a girlie magazine who brags about her 89-47-90 measurements will look stupid.*
> —Harold Blankenshire, Kanata

> *I disagree with the letter from Mr. Blankenshire of Kanata in yesterday's paper, both on his slurs of the great immigrants who are building our country and making it greater, not to mention a welcome increase in more ethnic restau-*

rants in Ottawa. Sir, a woman who "brags about her 89-47-90 measurements" would continue to look attractive. And you, by looking at her in your "girlie magazines," are hopelessly sexist.

—Ms. Mary Lou Krakowski, Tweed

I think all this garbage about metric-this and metric-that is so much hooey. It's not like they're shoving French down our throat.

—Dr. Ralph Cummings, Arnprior

I wrote to my Member of Parliament that he should shove the metric system where the sun doesn't shine, and his personal assistant wrote me yesterday saying that he didn't understand where that was. What kind of people are we electing to higher office, anyway?

—Paul Martin Jr.

A Gallup Poll taken in late 1983 showed just how successfully metrification in this country had taken hold in but a few short years. The number of Canadians between eighteen and twenty-nine years of age who found our nation's conversion to metric to be "very difficult" or "somewhat difficult" was only 62%, merely 73% of those between thirty and forty-nine, and an infinitesimal 80% of those over fifty. And what about the potential problems of going metric when our Best Friends to the South stayed imperial?

Okay, okay. So Canada went metric, gleefully changing 4,278,901 highway signs from miles to kilometres, a multi-billion-dollar make-work project for thousands of companies owned by Liberal Party members from coast to coast. But never before now has someone actually confronted the tremendous tensions and anguish created by two nations sharing the same continent but using two different measuring systems! American visitors to our beautiful country have become confused, annoyed, and just plain infuriated by the metrification of Canada. Let me share a few examples.

Mabel Finnigan of Kansas City has not seen her beloved nephew (on her late husband's side), Marvin Hanson, in Toronto for several years now. How on Earth is the family doing? The kids must be almost grown! So, in late July, Mabel calls her favourite relative with a view to an August visit.

"What's the temperature up there now, Marvin?"

"Oh, it's gorgeous, Auntie Mabel! It's been hovering in the high twenties all week."

Mabel hangs up her phone in horror, assuming that Marvin was referring to the same frigid Fahrenheit twenties that she suffers through every winter in Kansas City. Toronto, always billions in debt anyway, has just lost the hundreds of much-needed dollars that Mabel would have pumped into that city's flagging economy. A pre-SARS trauma, to say the least.

Bert Kowalski of Santa Cruz, California, is enjoying a delightful few days of endless rain in Vancouver, British Columbia, inspired by the view of Grouse Mountain during those rare moments when he can actually see through the dark clouds.

Bert feels a pang of hunger and spots a grocery store in the distance. There he sees the prices. Apples, $2.89/kg. Pears, $3.25/kg.

"Good heavens!" he thinks to himself, because Bert is not the type to use the Lord's name in vain even though it's being removed from his local schools. "How on Earth can Canadians afford food at these prices?"

Bert then notices a giant sign that declares "CHICKEN BREASTS ON SALE THIS WEEK: $3.95/KG." Back home chicken rarely costs over a dollar or two a pound. Bert runs out of the store, promising to adopt a Canadian child on the Foster Parent Plan just as soon as he gets back home.

Fred Putnam of Norfolk, Virginia, a safe and cautious driver for all of his seventy-three years, is on his way to Nova Scotia, which he hears is a lovely place to visit if not to live. He carefully observes the speed limit on the New York State Thruway and on into Canada, heading east toward the Maritimes.

Fred spots a sign: "100 KM PER HOUR." "KM?" he thinks to himself, scratching his head. Like most Americans, he lacks the curiosity to try to understand what those unknown letters refer to, but he certainly understands the number "100."

He floors the gas pedal on his Ford. Like all of his 300 million fellow citizens, he buys only American products, unless, of course, they are much cheaper if made elsewhere.

Poor Putnam is clocked by Ontario Provincial Police at ninety-eight miles an hour and receives a $240 fine (not realizing that this amount will equal only a handful of

U.S. dollars; such differences between the two great neigh-bours work both ways, you know). Putnam vows never to return to this strange country, and our tourism industry suffers accordingly.

Who needs the West Nile virus?

CITIZEN, HEAL THYSELF

The United States and Canada have strongly differing opinions on health care. The former does not care if its citizens have it; the latter cares — but not to the point of spending the money to preserve it.

It is well known that some forty million Americans are without "adequate health care," which may be for the best since over 100,000 U.S. citizens die from wrongly prescribed medicines each year. Thanks to its national health care system, Canada makes sure that every citizen, regardless of age, gender, place of birth, language spoken, or sexual inclination (prone is best, according to most experts), receives what is now described as "inadequate health care."

A recent Ipsos Reid poll reveals just how satisfied Canadians are with their universal system.

- Fifty-two percent of Canadians say that they "think about the possibility of contracting a life-threatening illness at least once a month." (This probably increased in frequency to once an hour after SARS hit the airwaves, not to mention the hospitals, of much of Canada, especially Ontario.)
- Fifty percent of Canadians say that they are "eating better" to reduce their chances of contracting a life-threatening illness; for

example, they are switching to a diet coke with that Tim Horton's doughnut to cut down on caloric intake.

● Sixty-six percent of Canadians would "investigate and use alternative or non-traditional medicines even if [their] doctor was against the idea." Whether or not this has to do with figuring out that the Latin word iatrogenic scrawled by doctors on their records means "doctor caused" no one knows for sure.

● The Internet has become important to the vast majority of Canadians. Two out of three go on-line to discover health information, an even greater percentage than those who send joke e-mails (59%), use instant messaging (54%), bank on-line (49%), comparison shop (45%), or make a purchase (43%). The only higher uses are for Helping Out That Poor Nigerian General and Getting His Money out of His War-Torn Country (86%) and calling up "dirty pictures" (99%).

● Eighty-two percent of Canadians believe that their country's health-care system is "in a crisis," of which 61% base their opinion "on personal experience and not just hearsay." Interestingly, 62% of Canadians believe that there is enough funding in the system but that "it's just not getting to where it needs to be." Sort of like blood to the loins, which is why 93% of Canadians have taken advantage of those ubiquitous Viagra ads on the web.

● According to a report from Canada's Fraser Institute, what Canadians find most troublesome is the stunning increase in waiting times between referral and treatment. For instance, in 1993 Canadians waited an average of nineteen weeks for orthopedic surgery but thirty-three weeks a decade later; fourteen weeks for opthalmology in 1993 and twenty-six weeks in 2003; and thirteen weeks for neurosurgery in 1993 and eighteen weeks in 2003. Most tellingly, Canadian women who waited eight weeks for gynecological treatment in 1993 waited sixteen weeks a decade later. This only underlines how patient a people we Canadians are, even women in labour.

● The upside of Canada's deteriorating health-care system: unnecessary surgery has fallen 68% over the past decade as frustrated Canadians have gone on to heal themselves.

CRIME AND PUNISHMENT

The justice systems in the two countries are yet another way to place a spotlight on our differences. In the United States, in 2003, the Supreme Court ruled that a man who stole a few children's videotapes for his nieces would be jailed for the next fifty years without parole because it was his third violation. This was a result of the very popular "three strikes and you're out" clause in California, a misnomer because it's really "three strikes and you're *in*."

Yet, to avoid appearances of favouritism toward the poor, Americans refuse to prosecute, much less fine or jail, the CEOs of billion-dollar firms who have stolen hundreds of millions of dollars from the stock-buying public and have left thousands of their own employees without jobs or pensions.

Canada has its own way of serving the cause of justice. For instance, in the cases of Steven Truscott, Donald Marshall, and David Milgaard, the judges and juries sent young men to prison for life for crimes that they had not committed. But in the interest of even-handedness, Canada also has young-offender laws, which allow teenagers under a certain age not to have their names mentioned in the press and then literally to get away with murder.

Now which system would get *your* vote?

CONVICTS AND THE BALLOT BOX

On the subject of voting, in November 2002 the Supreme Court of Canada ruled that federal inmates — from murderers to bank robbers to pedophiles — are "morally worthy" to vote in federal elections. The 5-4 decision struck down a law that had prohibited most federal prisoners from voting. And so, for the first time in history, many thousands of convicted criminals will be able to cast a vote in the next federal election, when they will have the choice of voting Liberal, Liberal, or Liberal.

In the United States, convicts do **not** have the right to vote. The ethical and moral reasons behind the American decision are logical. If that country were to let the prisoners vote, this mainly poor, lower-class, visible minority constituency would cast their ballots for the Democrats. And since the Republicans are usually hardest on crime, and wish dearly for George W. Bush to win a second term in the fall of 2004, the law isn't about to change.

HANG 'EM HIGH

When it comes to capital punishment, there are sometimes surprising connections between the policies of Canada and the United States. For instance, the number forty. Canada last executed someone just over forty years ago, in December 1962. The United States executes someone every forty seconds. Or so. Some of them actually guilty.

Yet there are some key differences. For instance, when Pierre Trudeau essentially put an end to capital punishment in Canada, many Canadians were upset and wrote angry letters to the editors of their local newspapers. And when

George Ryan, shortly before leaving the governor's office of Illinois in 2003, commuted all the death penalties in his state, out of fear that several innocent men could be put to death, half the citizens of the state seriously began to threaten to execute *him*. In fact, since the United States brought back the death penalty in the late 1970s, over one hundred inmates across that country facing execution were exonerated of their capital crimes, often years after their convictions, usually because of DNA evidence. Alas, this is more complex in West Virginia and several southern states where everyone has the same DNA.

But those are only the exceptions that prove the rule in the minds of the vast majority of Americans in favour of capital punishment. Why should facts get in the way of justice? The homicide rate has not increased in any of the dozen U.S. states that have abolished capital punishment, but that is a worthless statistic to the pro-death penalty forces. Actually, such forces in Canada (though far smaller and less powerful) show the same indifference to real evidence. Since Canada ended the death penalty in 1976, the annual homicide rate has declined precipitously from 3.09 per 100,000 people to 1.80.

The Supreme Court of each country has its own say in the matter. In early 2002, for instance, the highest U.S. court ordered an end to the execution of mentally retarded killers for the highly moral and ethical reason that "the public consensus in favor of this practise no longer exists." Clearly, Americans are turning into bleeding hearts after all these years, possibly due to the dangerous influence of the pinkos north of them.

And Canada? Well, in the fall of 2002, its Supreme Court agreed to review Section 43 of the Criminal Code, which states that "spanking, when used judiciously and with restraint, is an option that has its place."

Americans fret over putting people (whether guilty or innocent) to death; Canadians wonder if they should criminalize spanking. One more difference between the two nations worth pondering.

POTHEAD NATION

Canada and the United States have moved further apart on the question of whether marijuana should be decriminalized or even legalized. Recent polls in Canada have shown that 70% of its citizens are in favour of recreational drugs being legalized. Recent polls in the United States have shown that 100% of its citizens are in favour of these drugs being legalized, but all of those interviewed were in prison for buying, selling, or possessing pot. As for the rest of the country, less than 40% think that it should be legal.

In the summer of 2002, a special committee of the Canadian Senate produced a six-hundred-page report recommending the legalization of marijuana. (It was originally over a thousand pages, but several of the senators got the munchies and ate nearly half of the document.) These senators — a lawyer, an oil exec, an insurance broker, a realtor, and a professional musician (ha!), ranging in age from fifty-three to seventy-three — argued that pot is less habit forming than alcohol or cigarettes; that physical and psychological addiction is rare; that smoking pot does not lead to using harder drugs; and that, to quote the musician, "the shit coming out of British Columbia over the past few years is, like, really, uh, groovy."

The Senate report estimated that some three million Canadians between the ages of fourteen and sixty-five had smoked pot in the previous year, yet only twenty thousand are arrested on cannabis possession charges each year, which is even worse than Canadian Alliance voting percentages east of Alberta.

Americans, on the other hand, believe that marijuana is a dangerous drug: habit forming, addictive, and a gateway to harder drugs. Worst of all, it could lead to voting for left-wing candidates. Americans also spend several billion a year on law enforcement and have given criminal records to many millions of Americans who are probably liberals anyway.

Meanwhile, should Canada legalize pot, certain things will likely happen: tourism to Canada from the United States will probably increase exponentially, as will car accidents on the way home, and, not coincidentally, the U.S. government will probably begin to bomb Canadian cities. To quote President Bush, "Just say 'No,' Canada, **or else**."

NOTE ON THE SUBJECT OF FIREARMS

In early 2003, an eastern Ontario school board, having received a complaint from a student, removed the word *gun* from all spelling tests in its schools. By coincidence, in the same week, several dozen Americans in nine U.S. states sued their local school boards because their kids were not allowed to bring in Daddy's gun for show and tell.

PART 6

Crossing the Longest (Formerly) Undefended Border in the World

CANADIAN AND AMERICAN
RESPONSES TO 9/11

People respond to difficult situations in different ways, of course. One man may hear a strange tapping on his living room window in Brandon, Manitoba, and call 911. Another man may hear a similarly strange tapping on his St. Louis, Missouri, window, reach for his handgun, and send his second cousin Herb, on a surprise visit from Tallahassee, to an early meeting with his ancestors and a chance to check out the afterlife. But do these responses really have anything to do with the nationalities of the people involved?

Some would say yes; others would say probably.

Both countries have experienced invasion — Canada by the United States in the War of 1812, when Canadian and British soldiers soon pushed the Americans back across the border, and the United States by a few Middle Eastern types in 2001, an attack to which it reacted in the only way one would expect from the most powerful nation on Earth: shredding of their constitutional rights, hysteria, mass panic, racist attacks on its own citizens who looked too tanned or wore Sikh turbans, and thoughtful preparation to avoid future attacks.

To be fair to our American neighbours (oh, they make it hard), this invasion may have lasted only a few hours, but it did occur in two important cities and far more recently than the invasion of Canada. Thus, it is still fresh in their minds.

And so, to illustrate the ways that Canadians and Americans react to terrorism, here are selections from brochures about self-protection, reprinted with permission from each country.

Canada, Terrorism, and You: Be Prepared!

We in Canada have recently witnessed barbaric, un-Canadian-like attacks inflicted on the United States of America. There appears to be a definite threat to the West, and, according to top scholars of international relations whom we in the government have contacted, Canada is part of the West. Here are some actions that you, as a responsible Canadian citizen, can take to protect yourself and your loved ones, both at home and away from home.

1. Wear a pin that displays the Canadian flag clearly on your person, preferably on your lapel or blouse.
2. Purchase a large sticker of a red maple leaf, or of our flag, and place it on all your luggage should you be travelling out of the country.
3. Place your wallet in a safe place, preferably in a front pocket of your jeans or slacks. If you wish to take the great risk of putting your wallet into a back pocket, then choose one that has a button on it so that you can protect your wallet better.
4. If you hear of any new attacks on American cities, return to your home at once and watch CBC. CNN will probably be overly sympathetic to the American cause, and, as Canadians, we

must always be seen as even-handed; think of our history as peacekeepers. You may wish to check out CTV or even Global (although the latter is overly sympathetic to the American cause, owned as it is by the same people who publish the right-wing the *National Post*; think twice about the latter). You can always try Newsworld.

5. If you are confronted by anyone and accused of being an American — whether on the streets of Canada, the United States, or overseas, proudly flash your lapel/blouse pin and declare "I am Canadian/Je suis un(e) Canadien(ne)." Doing so improves your chances of survival by a factor of ten. Blood-thirsty terrorists may not like us very much, but everyone knows they've got a real bee in their bonnet over the Yankees, for whatever reasons. Some CSIS managers think that this has to do with reality TV, but the planning of 9/11 appears to have begun before those shows hit the international airwaves.

6. Remember: never hide the fact that you are a Canadian: innocuous, dull, unassuming, your eyes firmly planted on your pension. These simple truths could save your life.

—The Minister of Defence in Ottawa

THE FINE ART OF AIR TRAVEL

In this post-9/11 world, travel to the United States, particularly by air, has become far more difficult. Even so, Canadians insist on going south for holidays (those discount packages to Miami are hard to resist), sightseeing (Mardi Gras!), business, and visiting those relatives who were foolish enough to remain American during the Vietnam War or have moved there for salaries twice what they could earn in Canada. So, in the interest of smoother relations between our nations, and in the hope of easing the experience of Canadians passing through American airports and dealing with American officials, I reprint the following brochure from the U.S. Office of Homeland Security. Originally intended for American citizens, this advice can easily be adapted to the Canadian traveller who wishes for a more stress-free trip to the great country to the south.

ARRIVING AT THE AIRPORT

Remember one simple rule: the less time you spend in this dangerous environment, the better. Note the very word *terminal*, usually associated with fatal disease.

Until 9/11 occurred, most wise Americans arrived at the last minute, even seconds before their planes were about to depart. Today, however, speak and walk slowly from the moment you walk through the deadly, far too quickly closing automatic doors. Shuffle your feet, but do this quietly. This simple act saved the lives of hundreds of thousands of American black people in the South over many decades.

Keep your eyes lowered at all times. The head of Homeland Security informed us that he once found a quarter this way, although it was covered with germs, and he was later sorry that he'd picked it up. And never forget to wear the buttons that your leaders in Washington, DC, mailed to you along with this brochure. Yes, always wear your "PLEASE DON'T SHOOT! I'M AN AMERICAN" button, printed in a dozen languages. In fact, you should pin it on even before setting foot outside your front door.

Here are a few rules for you to memorize before going to an airport.

- *Do not look like a celebrity*. Terrorists hate celebrities since they see them on Al-Jazeera and get even more jealous than when they see Coca-Cola machines, McDonald's restaurants, or Starbucks stores, which are all threatening reminders of the worldwide success of capitalism and the worldwide failure of godless communism and God-obsessed Islam.
- *Do not look like a successful businessperson*, thus earning the wrath, not to mention the anger, of a jealous, impoverished terrorist from a Fourth or Fifth World country.
- *Do not look like an American politician* of either party.
- *Do not look like a First (or Second) World politician*.
Remember that it was the pope and John Lennon who got shot

and not the papal nuncio or Yoko Ono; nobodies are usually ignored in this world, thank heaven. Think of your father's favourite grand-nephew; he turned out to be a nobody, but he also died a natural death, did he not?

What if you lose something at the airport, such as your ticket, memory, money, mind, or credit card? Rush to the traveller's aid booth, usually located at some impossible-to-find location. Be aware that the elderly woman within that booth is as clueless as you are. She landed that volunteer job barely an hour ago, when her niece got sick and called her to fill in. She is unsure which city she is in, much less how to help *you*. But she is trying her best, which is more than you'll be able to say about the people who made the meals for your flight should you ever get on board. Do be polite and sympathetic, like all good Americans usually are. Never forget that this woman managed to reach her nineties; what are your chances of doing the same?

The following advice is crucial.

How do you know when you are in the wrong lineup at the airport?
- You are surrounded by a Burmese dance troupe.
- You are surrounded by young children wearing uniforms and wooden shoes and speaking a strange language that sounds a bit like Yiddish.
- The line moves quickly.
- The line flows out of the airport terminal that you recently entered, and the people in front of you eagerly climb into a limousine.

- The line flows out of the terminal that you just entered, and you are crammed into a bus heading back into the city where you live.

How do you know when you are in the correct lineup at the airport?
- You have not moved for ninety minutes.
- You are surrounded by screaming babies held by mothers trying to shove bottles into their mouths.
- You are surrounded by scruffy men openly and illegally smoking, carrying huge placards that read *"Yeah, I'm smoking. You want to make something of it, Buddy? Has everyone forgotten about the 26th Amendment?"*

One of the great things about the United States is that it allows all kinds of extreme religious and political groups to express themselves freely. Terrorists hate Americans for this, as you know. More than any other nation on God's Earth, the United States recognizes the crucial importance of freedom of speech. This means that every extreme religious and political group is present in every American airport from California to New York, from Minnesota to Texas, and you'll quickly become familiar with spiritual concepts that range from human sacrifice to polytheism and political concepts from left of Mao to right of Mussolini, as far as Rush Limbaugh. You can learn much from these experiences, all of which will strengthen your desire to defend America in general, and your family and loved ones in particular, against Ruthless Terrorists and Evildoers.

Here are some tips.

● If the people who accost you at the airport are Hare Krishnas, you have a number of options. If you choose to give them money, they will gratefully perform their entire dance and prayer ritual. This may lead to your missing your plane, which could be for the best.

● If you do not give these people your money, they will pursue you onto your plane with as much vigour and tenacity as Javert tracking Jean Valjean.

● If the person who accosts you at the airport is a supporter of Lyndon Larouche or David Duke, and hands you bumper stickers that read "NUKE AL GORE," "MAKE WAR, NOT LOVE," "SLAVERY NEVER TOOK PLACE, AND YOU KNOW IT," "JESUS WAS NOT A JEW," or "SEND BILL COSBY BACK TO AFRICA," you have the right to either accept or reject this generous offer.

You may also be confronted by panhandlers at the airport. What to do in these terrorist-ridden times?

● You may wish to give the poor fellow a subway token.

● You may wish to give the person a token of your appreciation.

● You may wish to share with him or her some of the fascinating pamphlets and bumper stickers that you just received from those zealous, Constitution-supported followers of Lyndon Larouche, David Duke, or Hare Krishna.

● Do not be surprised to discover that the panhandler is incorporated and carries a cell phone to talk with subpanhandlers who are part of his multilevel marketing scheme spread throughout other areas of the airport. He may even offer you a franchise in his company.

You have finally reached the front of the check-in counter at the airport, and we recommend the following.

- Say "I'm from Canada." The reason is obvious: no one, except other Canadians, really hates people who are Canadian. Especially the terrorists who have flowed into that dull nation over the past few decades — they love the place. Canadians stand for nothing, which means that they will stand for anything. Even public office. Just say "I'm from Canada!" and leave it at that. Should they ask to see your passport and you are not, of course, a Canadian, just tell them that you left it in the cab, which they'd expect to hear from that bleeding-heart, Cuba-loving nation.
- When at the counter, never make eye contact with anyone, even your own spouse.
- Do not make flamboyant hand gestures, which means that Italians, Jews, Greeks, and other Mediterranean types would do well to take the train, even if they are travelling to Europe, Asia, or — are they nuts? — the Middle East.
- Do not show flashy business cards, such as Gold American Express. As the head of the CIA likes to joke, "Please — please — *leave* home without it." Toys Я Us and Costco credit cards are strongly recommended.
- Watch out for anyone wearing a turban, kafiya, dagger, djellaba, fez, monocle, or submachine gun.
- Report to the airport authorities anyone who looks suspicious, even members of your own family.
- Certain things must never be said at an airport, especially to an El Al agent.
    - "My grandma packed my bags" (especially if you are over sixty-five).

- "This should be a blast."
- "I've always wanted to visit Libya, and today I finally have my chance."
- "I really love it when they gun the plane on takeoff."
- "Hi, Jack!" (to a friend who goes by that name).
- Wash your hands exceedingly carefully after feeding your dog before leaving for the airport. There is nothing like the taunting smell of Dr. Ballard to tease those airport dogs right out of their leashes.

This is really important to remember: after September 11th, irony is dead. So is comedy, at least at airports. If the metal detector goes off as you pass through it, we strongly advise against using any of the following lines.

- "Damn it! I forgot to turn off my pacemaker!" (especially if you are a teenager or younger).
- "It's only shrapnel; just ignore it."
- "I just *knew* that my dentist has been using too much mercury to fill my cavities."
- "I've got this metal plate in my head; wanna hear the story behind it?"
- "Okay, okay, your damned machine caught me. Now just stand back with your hands on your heads, and nobody is gonna get hurt."

Should you have cried out any of the above or similar stupidities, it is time for the *strip search*. Obey the following advice closely.

- Do not be nervous.
- Do not object or complain.

- You cannot forestall this, especially after 9/11. Screaming out lines such as "My uncle is Alan Dershowitz" or "My stepdad is Johnnie Cochran" or "I know who *really* killed JFK" or, worst of all, "I know which U.S. federal government officials were truly behind September 11th" will only work against you.

To be frank, a strip search can be enjoyable, even thrilling. The guards often have warm hands. Indeed, a strip search could well be the highlight of your entire trip and has sometimes led to a meaningful relationship with authorities.

You have now reached the departure lounge and are waiting for your plane to take off. You cannot go back now. You have passed the Point of No Return. This is it. We have reports of pregnant women who have given birth in departure lounges because the guards, ever vigilant since 9/11, would not let them back into the main terminal.

You are now literally and physically stuck, waiting for a plane that may never leave. And even if it does take off, it may take you to a foreign land where they don't know enough to speak English. Which includes much of New York, now that we think of it.

PART 7

Fun and Games

OUR NATIONAL SPORTS

Sports can tell us a great deal about a country and its citizens. For instance, the national game of the United States has always been considered to be baseball, even though it was superseded by football several years ago and now by basketball, since Americans love to be entertained by black people, who seem to be less threatening on a playing field or court than on the street. Nightclubs are OK, too.

Canada's official sport is lacrosse, even though hardly anyone aside from private-school girls has played it. But the true, if unofficial, national game of Canada is curling. To gain further insight into the two different nations that share the North American continent, here are brief studies of their "national games."

THE ALL-AMERICAN GAME: BASEBALL

Baseball is a contest between two teams of nine players each, the best of them from Cuba, the Dominican Republic, or Japan. It involves the throwing, batting, and catching of a ball on a field on which are placed four bases at fixed points, assuming that the regular strike talks between players and team owners have been settled by the time each game begins.

The most skilled players in amateur baseball usually go professional for the sheer love of the game and the $14-million-a-year salary. They make the sport their full-time vocation from late February until early October each year unless they belong to the New York Yankees, who play until November every fall since the team can afford to purchase the costly services of the best players of each era.

At its core, baseball is a simple sport with no more rules than, say, the Muslim or Jewish religion. Two teams of nine players each, under the direction of a manager (who will not be fired, by revered tradition, until the team that he is managing loses four games in a row), play on an enclosed field surrounded by boisterous, often drunk fans who have paid six bucks for each plastic cup of warm beer. Regulation baseball games usually last three and a half to four hours, considered poetic since, unlike football or basketball, baseball is not limited by time, merely by the completion of nine innings. More important, longer games mean that dozens of extra commercials can be squeezed into the radio and TV broadcast. This disregard of time has led to baseball inspiring the finest authors and journalists in North America to write exquisitely, as no other sport manages to do, a fact that thrills its thousands of fanatical fans across North America, even though most of them cannot or will not read.

After George Steinbrenner purchased the New York Yankees and, due to his bottomless wealth, the World Series nearly every year for the past decade, baseball has no longer been a competitive sport. Still, billions of dollars are spent by the eagerly betting public, led by one Pete Rose, who wager small fortunes on which date each year the major-league players will walk out in a contract dispute.

CANADA'S NATIONAL SPORT: CURLING

Aside from dodging mosquitoes or falling icicles in Winnipeg, curling is Canada's most exciting sport. It entails two teams of four players each sending stones along an ice surface toward a target circle, trying to land them closest to the centre. This aim differs greatly from that of Canada's other national sport, in which two teams of six players each send each other into the boards along an ice surface, trying to cripple the opponent, and in which the only stones are thrown by the spectators, along with pennies, live octopi, and rubber chickens. Go figure.

Curling as we know it was created in Scotland, a game for which, along with golf, that country should never be forgiven. The sport was initially played outdoors, until the cold weather made the brooms stick to the roofs of the players' mouths. The players soon moved to indoor facilities, which were quickly taken over by hockey goons who drove the curlers out of the buildings, forcing them to build their own.

Over the past century and more, many famous Canadians were fans of curling, ranging from Sir John A. Macdonald to Lord Dufferin. The latter even had a rink built — at his own expense for a change, unlike, say, Pierre Trudeau's pool — at Rideau Hall, his official residence at the time. Perhaps the greatest curling fan in the twentieth century was Premier Robert Bourassa of Quebec, who even had his own hairdresser to do his curls. In recent decades,

Winnipeg has become the centre of the sport, with far more clubs than in Toronto and Montreal. This is why Winnipegers are constantly moving to either Toronto or Montreal; they are trying to forget about the sport entirely.

Today dozens of men and women play this fascinating, soporific sport regularly. All that is needed to play are a sliding shoe (preferably two), a few corn brooms, hand savers, brushes, gloves, polyester slacks and sweater, and dozens of stones, which altogether cost only a few hundred thousand dollars. This is why the game has caught on with rich Canadians. And what pleasures does curling provide? (Sadly, that is a rhetorical question.) Curling has provided so many Canadians with countless hours of fun just trying to figure out what on Earth is happening down there. From the "flat-footed slide," which the entire federal Progressive Conservative Party perfected from 1984 to the present, to the cleaning of the stone, to the positioning of the throwing arm, to the positioning of the broom arm, to the positioning of the head and body, to the "in-turn grip," to the grippe caught in chilly rinks, to the function and position of the hack leg, to the trailing leg and toe position, to the follow-through — curling has baffled billions while entertaining hundreds of others.

Which other sport has gotten so many Canadians — including a number who are not even Scottish — to sweep together? And how many other Canadians over the decades have been warned not to sweep together until they are married?

Thanks to this wildly popular sport, dozens of charming terms have entered the everyday vocabulary of millions of Canadians: *Biter. Bland end. Back-board weight. Burned stone. Chip-and-roll. Draw weight. Hack weight. Hog line. Keen ice. Dead handle. Shot rock. Skip. Swingy ice. Tee line. Vice skip. Wick. Wrecked shot.* And many others too numerous and stupid to mention.

Curling. If only the participants got their teeth knocked out and their ribs broken, it could eventually become the most popular sport in Canada. Until then, it will remain on TSN from 3:00 to 4:30 a.m. every other Tuesday to fulfil Canadian content regulations.

A note to end this discussion of curling: in the spring of 2003, the Canadian Curling Association joined with the Canadian Dental Association in the twentieth annual cosponsorship of their **Brush Regularly!** campaign.

A NOTE ON
SOVEREIGNTY AND SPORTS

Canada's other national game is hockey, but it involves fast-moving, quick-thinking, skilful players and thus doesn't seem to reflect the Canadian spirit. On second thought, the 1,450 teams that currently comprise the National Hockey League are made up more and more of players from Czechoslovakia, Sweden, the former Soviet Union, and a dozen other foreign countries. So the game is more reflective of Canada than ever before.

Canada has survived two world wars, the near separation of its French-speaking province and threats of separation from several others, gays in the military, taxes heavier than Oprah before her latest diet. But never has it suffered an indignity greater than one that occurred early in the new century: *the Montreal Canadiens hockey team, one of the Original Six, is now owned by an American.* If Canada only had real armed forces, this would mean war.

PASS ME A COLD ONE:
BEER IN CANADA

Brewing is a major industry in Canada, with dozens of conventional breweries and many smaller ones, including brew pubs, operating across the country, employing tens of thousands of citizens and inebriating millions more.

Beer making was common among the earliest traders and settlers; since it was so cold most of the time, pioneers demanded a palatable antifreeze. Moreover, offering an "unfriendly brew" to the Natives was a great way of keeping them quiet. Still works.

"Beer" changes its meaning, of course, depending on where you live in Canada. In Quebec, it's against the law to call it anything but *bière*, which means "ale." In western Canada, "beer" means "lager," and asking for *bière* there will label you as "a frog from the east."

The production, distribution, and sale of beer in Canada adds billions to our gross national product, with tens of millions of dollars spent on barley, malt, hops, and other agricultural products, not to mention car repair and hospital bills. If it were not for Canadian beer, much of this healthy grain would have been sent to some African nation or other, where the people would actually have eaten the stuff.

Most important, Canadian beer is higher in alcoholic content than American beer, has led to more teenagers driving from U.S. border towns into Canada than anything else, including casinos and the downtown Vancouver streetwalkers.

BEER IN THE UNITED STATES

When Canada was still mainly wilderness (sort of like Thunder Bay today), Virginia colonists were brewing ale out of corn. But within two decades, the first shipments of beer arrived from England. Americans being Americans (even seventeen decades before they actually became "Americans"), they were bringing brewers over from London by 1609 and had established a brewery in New Amsterdam (later Manhattan) by 1612.

I could fill this book with the importance of beer to the American economy and people, listing giant brewers such as Anheuser-Busch, Miller, and Coors, but what it all comes down to is a single verifiable fact: to Canadians, American beer tastes like soda pop.

American Claims of Canadian Assets

Canadians have often complained that Americans have been too eager to claim the products of our country, whether actors, singers, or oil, as their own. Which complaining is silly, of course, because Canadians eagerly sold off each of them anyway, like any good whore.

But the last straw, in the minds of many Canadians, was when singer-songwriter Joni Mitchell was honoured with a two-hour special on the esteemed PBS television series *American Masters* early in 2003. Ms. Mitchell, as every Canadian over the age of ten and perhaps ten Americans know so well, was born, raised, and made her fame in Canada.

But this appropriation is understandable when one keeps in mind that the vast majority of Americans also believe that capital punishment means safer streets, that tax breaks for the rich will eventually assist the poor, and that President Bush was democratically elected in 1999.

BEAUTIFUL WORDS:
OUR COUNTRY'S LITERATURE

Saul Bellow lives in Chicago, but he was born in Quebec, which makes him the first almost Canadian to win the Nobel prize for literature. Carol Shields was an American-born Canadian, which made her the only Canuck to win the Pulitzer Prize. John Irving is definitely from New England, but he married a Toronto woman and has set parts of *A Prayer for Owen Meany* and *Son of a Circus* there. These three authors have been claimed by both countries; do they belong to them or us?

One Canadian writer who has gone strangely unclaimed by the Americans (except for Oprah Winfrey, who had him on her show) is Rohinton Mistry. One of our most respected and successful novelists, the mild-mannered Mistry cancelled the second half of his last U.S. book tour, complaining that he faced "unbearable humiliation" as a result of racial profiling at every American airport in which he landed. As a representative of his U.S. publisher, Alfred A. Knopf, wrote in a memo to bookstores, "As a person of colour he was stopped repeatedly and rudely at each airport along the way. . . ." Mistry complained at a time when the United States had begun to fingerprint, photograph, and register

Canadian citizens who'd originated in Muslim countries. Mistry comes from the rare Mohammedan sect Parsi.

The potential danger to national security that Mistry poses is yet another point of literary dispute between Canada and the United States. However, when it comes to literature, there is at least one thing that the citizens of both countries can agree on. *The English Patient* is pretty much unreadable both north and south of the forty-ninth parallel.

TRASH TIDINGS

Much can upset the affection between nations. For instance, the War of 1812, when the Americans invaded Canada with the expressed purpose of taking the whole place over, weather and all. Or Canada's welcoming over ten thousand Vietnam resisters during that war, just as it had welcomed thousands of runaway slaves during the 1850s and 1860s. Well, accepted them.

But sometimes the disaffection can be caused by something far less, such as the fact that, since January 1, 2003, 130 trucks have been carrying most of Toronto's trash every day to an area just south of Detroit named Sumpter Township. Actually, trash has been migrating from Toronto to this three-stoplight town for several years but never more than in 2003, when some 1.2 million tons of Canadian garbage will be dumped into the American landfill. The added trash has moved Michigan to second place among states that import trash, up from third, ahead of Virginia and behind Pennsylvania. Not gold, but silver at least.

There is growing resentment among the local American population, some of whom dare to suggest that Canadian garbage does not smell like roses. This kind of anti-Canadian attitude is far more typical among Albertans referring to Ottawa or Quebec, but it still occurs in the United States today in spite of our centuries-old friendship. Little can be done, however. Under the North American Free Trade Agreement (NAFTA), the movement of trash across the Canada-U.S. border is no different from the *interstate* movement of trash.

Still, it's an ill wind. This new cross-border tension has led to a renaissance of popular poetry. A small group of opponents in a town near the new Michigan landfill recently rewrote the Elvis Presley hit "Return to Sender":

Send us bacon and hockey,
    Beer and curling, too.
But if you send us your garbage,
    We'll send it right back to you.
    And write upon it:
Return to sender,
Address Unknown.

If Canada were to take in **American** trash, no doubt protestors would begin with a slightly more relevant song to parody, such as Ian Tyson's "Four Strong Winds."

Meanwhile, up in Canada, it has been noted by experts that Michigan sent Canada fifty-three thousand tons of hazardous waste last year and received only four thousand tons from its northern buddy. Typical.

Furthermore, the Americans have sent us billions of tons of garbage over the radio and on TV and movie screens for the past century, and Céline Dion can hardly be seen as an equivalent payback. OK, OK, Alanis maybe.

Sumpter Township has about twelve thousand residents spread over thirty-seven square miles crisscrossed by dirt roads. On the outskirts of the community, near the Toronto-supplied garbage dump, a brightly painted sign describes the town as "COUNTRY LIVING AT ITS FINEST." And, indeed, the bulging, snowcapped hill at the landfill could be mistaken for a sledder's paradise, except for the overwhelming stench and the endless row of trucks every day.

If Canada had a similar dump, nearby residents would undoubtedly put up a sign reading "Sorry about the dump, but they paid us big bucks to take it on. And the smell should be gone within a few centuries." Clearly, Canadians have a lot to learn about advertising.

ADOPT-A-CHILD, UNITED STATES; ADOPT-A-CHILD, CANADA

In my attempt to discover the differences between the two great nations of North America, I came across ads for Adopt-a-Child, a fine organization that works in over one hundred nations. Although we tend to think that nonprofit groups such as Adopt-a-Child are primarily focused on impoverished countries such as Haiti, Ethiopia, and the ever-popular Burkina Faso, it is not so. Perhaps you can glean from the fund-raising pleas below how different Canada and the United States are when it comes to needy children.

CANADIAN CHILDREN NEED YOUR HELP!
Over the past year, and for many decades now, Adopt-a-Child has been helping Canadian children who cry out for our assistance. Did you know the following frightening facts?

- Housing for Canada's children is almost unaffordable, especially in cities such as Vancouver and Toronto. In the 1960s, barely four decades ago, a modest home could be purchased by the parents or foster parents of a Canakid (as we lovingly and condescendingly call them) for a mere $30,000; today the same two-bedroom, one-bathroom home can cost as much as

$500,000 in a good neighbourhood. How can these children afford to live in decent, clean environments?

● Adopt-a-Child has struggled for years to assist the worst kind of famine across Canada: children who live on *poutine* — a nearly inedible dairy product that the Québécois tribe somehow manages to ingest; others across the mostly uninhabitable country who struggle to survive on Timbits, an unhealthy, deep-fried product that produces more gas than the country's once-owned, now-sold energy industries; and those who live on MSG dumped into the food of millions of recent immigrants to Canada from the Far East, causing stomach upset, weakened colon walls, and more.

● Monsoon rains fall endlessly across the westernmost province of Canada, leaving millions marooned — trapped between a giant ocean to the west and towering mountains to the east. Rain in Richmond and Squamish, British Columbia, has run up to 387 consecutive days. The endless precipitation leads to massive depression and even suicide among the parents of the miserable children of this province and among some senior politicians, some of whom have turned to alcohol.

● Clean water has been a tragic problem for villages and towns in Canada, such as Walkerton in the middle of the country. Children have actually died from innocently drinking well water, a tragedy usually not encountered outside Third World nations, which at least have warm weather to compensate.

● Over the past several years, the comically named "loonie" and "toonie" of Canada, along with the colourful paper currency, have collapsed in value and are worth little more than half of what they were but a few decades ago. This devaluation has made travelling out of this long-frozen land nearly impossible for children and their struggling parents.

● The children of "the rock," as their far eastern area is known, are especially hard hit. The major industry, cod, has been depleted to the vanishing point, leaving the impoverished parents of the poor children of this area to rely entirely on rapidly decreasing government aid. Furthermore, the children of New-Found-Land, as this area is called, are taunted and ridiculed by cruel jokes from both children and adults across the rest of this snow-capped country. Here's my favourite: "A woman is mugged, and her purse is stolen. She finds her way to the police, who question her and then place her in a darkened room. Five men parade across a stage in front of the poor victim, and the suspect in the middle — a 'Newfie,' as these easterners are called — suddenly points to the woman complainant and cries out, 'That's *her*!'" Such jokes are a vicious, cruel mockery that these poor children must live with until their parents are sadly forced to move to the "Boston area" in a totally different country to the south.

● Even in the political realm, Canadian children are suffering as they see literal "jokes" elected to higher office, especially in the two most western provinces of this geographically challenged land.

● The entire country that these children are tragically born into — or migrate to, which is even more pathetic — is bitter cold for much of the year. A heartbreaking proverb of this benighted land goes "There are four seasons in this country: fall, winter, winter, and winter." In the Prairies, the middle portion of the land, the seasons purportedly number five: "mosquitoes, winter, winter, winter, and winter."

● The children of Canada are actually forced to learn a second language — something unknown in the far wealthier, more fortunate country just to its south — and, even worse, they must study metric, an obscure system that includes "kilopascals" and other such ancient absurdities.

● There are few freedoms left to these miserable creatures. For instance, the cruel laws of their land force them to listen on the radio to the music written by fellow Canadians, even when they long to hear the sounds of more enticing lands. These disagreeable rules, known as "can-con," have forced many children of Canada to turn to the Internet and radio stations from other countries to listen to what they actually enjoy. The same thing goes for much of what they see on television as well — forcing their parents to spend much of their already depleted income on cable and satellite dishes.

● Most Canadian children, especially those lucky enough to reach adolescence by not drinking the water, are oppressed by what is known as "PC," truly the disease of this frigid land. Unlike children in so many other countries around the world, they are denied the right to hear teachers speak freely about international Jewish conspiracies. They cannot even call Christmas trees by their rightful name but must refer to them as "holiday trees."

● As in too many other countries around the world, the children of Canada must see their mothers paid less than their fathers. Those unfortunate enough to live in the area known as "Quebec" cannot even go to the schools that they want to attend because the subjects taught are presented in the "wrong" language. Shockingly, there are actual "language police" who enforce such indignities.

● Perhaps saddest of all, the children of Canada are oppressed by some of the highest taxes in the world: there are harsh and overbearing federal taxes, abusive provincial taxes, and even municipal taxes, making the lives of their parents brutal and their own lives precarious.

The Children of the North (as they are called in both mockery and sympathy) need your help. Give soon and give often. *Canadian children need you like never before.*

AMERICAN CHILDREN NEED YOUR HELP

The children of the United States — known lovingly or comically as "Yankees" — are suffering like never before, and they need your money — or at least your sympathy. Adopt-a-Child is targeting these tens of millions of youngsters this year since they need assistance more than ever. Why? Take a look at these horrors.

- Across the United States, countless children are tortured by endless war, especially by watching the History Channel and being dragged to see Hollywood movies.
- Millions of American children are orphaned as their parents are forced to go off to work each morning or are divorced or both.
- In nearly every state of the union, Yankee youth are sent to jail for years for possessing an ounce or two of a minor drug, while rapists and murderers get off with a slap on the hand.
- Millions of American children are actually given sugar-coated cereals every morning, on which they sprinkle more sugar, making cereal manufacturers and diabetes doctors rich, while these pathetic creatures slowly, inevitably sink into physical degeneration.
- In many states, hundreds of thousands of American children of Hispanic background are denied the right to speak their native

tongue, especially if it is Spanish, because English is considered the only acceptable language to speak by the unilingual majority.

● Millions of children unfortunate enough to be born in the United States are drugged every morning by their parents and/or teachers with strange drugs such as Ritalin in order to keep them from acting up in class, even though, when their parents acted up in school, they were considered creative and entrepreneurial.

● Many children have no feeling of security, even in their class-rooms, because most of the other kids have guns, while they cannot afford one. Even worse, millions have their own guns (borrowed from Mommy's purse or Daddy's car) yet lack the right, being under the age of majority (ten), to purchase ammunition at the local 7-11.

● Millions of American children are taught to beg for poison every night, such as KFC and overcooked hamburger, by being offered toys and games as incentives and to make them believe that they are happy.

● In this purportedly wealthy, First World country, schools are so impoverished by the lack of public support that they need to receive funds from international firms such as Coca-Cola, which then receive the right to put their carbonated beverage machines in many hallways.

● In most American schools, youths of all ages — from kinder-garten (if it hasn't been cancelled because there is no money left from fighting overseas wars) through high school — are actually forced to wear ugly uniforms, such as baggy or cut-off jeans, too-tight blouses, and grotesquely wide and long "bell-bottom" slacks, and even have to show their navels shamelessly.

● Countless other youth have to hang around malls with "nothing to do" merely because there is nothing good on TV that night. Or, even more horrible, there *is* something good on TV that night, but their parents are too stupid to set the VCR.

● In spite of the supposed wealth of the United States, when millions of children get ill (see the references to sugared cereals, fried chicken and hamburgers, and soda pop above), their parents cannot afford to purchase medical care due to the public fear of "socialism."

● Worst of all, countless millions of American children suffer from insecure financial futures and hear their parents crying out in their sleep from hideous nightmares because of the horrific collapse of the Internet stocks in April 2000 and after. So many billionaires became only millionaires. So many millionaires dropped to only hundred-thousandaires overnight. These children — and their parents — had been raised to believe in WorldCom, Enron, Global Crossing, Adelphia, Tyco, and so many other exciting companies, even more than believing in God, and they lived to see their hopes and dreams crash terribly. Fortunately, some sold out early, but what about those who bought the shares from those who sold out early? And then, just when their faith in capitalism was near total collapse, they learned that even revered accounting firms, such as Arthur Andersen, were equally corrupt. Thank heaven that many giants of American industry, such as the CEO of Tyco, Dennis Kozlowski, made $62 million in 2001, including stock options. Former chairman of Enron, Ken Lay, collected nearly $200 million in compensation from his company until he resigned in January 2001. Global Crossing executives sold over $1.3 billion of their stock holdings from 1999 until November 2001, so not *everyone* lost in this miserable market. But for so many other American parents and their children, this financial confusion is almost too sad to contemplate.

As you can see, Adopt-a-Child has wisely chosen the United States as a prime country to fulfil its mandate: to make sure that tens of millions of suffering American children be sponsored and supported emotionally and spiritually, as well as financially, by you men and women out there who are fortunate enough to live in a Third World country.

If you choose to adopt a child, you can even write postcards to these Yankee youth — the U.S. Postal Service still works to a degree, although, after a few more years of free e-mail, who knows? — since you will be provided with their names and addresses. Sadly, you may never hear back from these pathetic creatures since most of them have been going to incompetent, under-funded schools across the country and have been pushed forward from grade to grade without learning to read and write and then graduating fraudulently, because if they didn't graduate their parents would sue the school system. Lawyers, along with CEOs, appear to be the only ones who make money anymore in that tragic land.

Please adopt a child in the United States! Children there have never needed your support more than now. Even if they don't realize it yet.

IN CONCLUSION, (F)EH?

As Canadians would say, paraphrasing a classic song, "What's it all about, Parindra?" (Alfie having moved to the United States recently to make a better living). It's a good question, one that has taken me this entire book to attempt to answer. Although Canada and the United States share a continent, there are still plenty of differences between their respective people, cultures, and nations.

Let's take religion, a subject happily worth dying for in most countries in the world but one that brings a yawn to most Canadians — and not only during the reverend's sermon. A research poll in 2002 found that religion was "important" to 60% of Americans, but only 30% of Canadians would use the same adjective to describe the centrality of faith in their lives. Fewer than five million Canadians identify themselves as members of the United and Anglican Churches — nearly the same number as those who describe themselves as "nonreligious." Not that those two churches stand for anything other than getting whites out of South Africa and gays into the priesthood.

In the United States, it's different. Every American president has ended every speech with "God bless America." In fact, President Clinton used to mumble that phrase when he finished spending afternoons with Ms. Lewinsky. In Canada, few if any politicians — federal, provincial, or even municipal — would even *think* of saying that God should bless Canada, knowing that if he/she/it had ever done so the country would have far better weather. Most Canadians aren't even sure that God is on our side, much less on this side of the forty-ninth parallel. Americans, on the other hand, put "IN GOD WE TRUST" on their coins and dollars, knowing that with God's help the Euro can be crushed overnight.

It wasn't always this way, of course; in the middle of the just-completed century, the Catholic Church still ran welfare and education in Quebec, while its great enemy, the Orange Order of Super-Protestantism in Ontario, was more popular than Molson and Labatt beer put together. But religion has been shucked off by the vast majority of Canadian citizens, who are aware that God may dwell in Chicago or Pittsburgh or Baton Rouge but hardly in Brandon. Abortion rights slid into Canadian law and use with little struggle (starting in Quebec, of all places; some scholars think that *"Je me souviens"* on La Belle Province's licence plates actually refers to "Never forget to use birth control"). And when the Lord's Prayer was quietly removed from 99% of public classrooms across Canada, not only was there a complete lack of picketing, rioting, and letter writing to politicians, but also everyone across our country wanted to include prayers to Krishna, Allah, Buddha, and a few hundred other less major gods/goddesses to avoid offending their next-door neighbours, who come from 241 countries where they were often prevented from worshipping those guys/gals/idols freely. This is Canadian multiculturalism at its most glorious, or most offensive, depending on whether you're from Ontario or Alberta. Go figure.

Or look at the differences between Canadians and Americans in terms of foreign relations. Canada wants to invite every citizen of every nation of the world to become Canadian, while the United States wants to bomb them all into submission. That difference of attitude certainly differentiates the two countries.

There are *some* similarities between our two nations, of course — for instance, foreign aid. The country that spends the lowest share of its gross national product on foreign aid today is the United States, which is surely understandable: all those jet fighters and bombs cost a lot. But Canada is the *second* lowest spender in the world on foreign aid, which is informative if not a bit surprising to those who thought our country likes to help others out.

In military defence — which is Yiddish for "Let's kill them before they may kill us; who knows what evil lurks in the minds of non-Christians?" — the United States, of course, spends by far the most. But Canada really isn't so awful in that respect; it is not the lowest spender on defence, as many right-wingers in this country may suspect. No, it's the *second* lowest spender in the world, just after another giant, Luxembourg. So, as you can see, we Canadians are not on the **exact** opposite side of the defence-spending spectrum.

The U.S. budget for military spending in 2003 is nearly $380 billion, six times what Russia will spend, a dozen times more than England will spend, and fifty-five times more than Canada will shell out. Fortunately, Americans are willing to do without a few minor things in order to rule the world, such as universities, public schools, welfare, and health care for the stupidly uninsured. Because of these huge military expenditures, Americans have run up a gigantic deficit, while Canada has a growing surplus of money, which it hardly knows where to waste. Yet Americans keep cutting taxes for the rich, while Canadians raise taxes for everyone, being equal opportunity tax raisers in ways that the Yankees simply cannot wrap their minds around. Indeed, big government grows in Canada, while it shrinks in the United States, proving that the True North Weak and Semi-Free is greater than its neighbour in at least one thing.

And what of recreational drugs? I wanted to dedicate a full chapter to this contentious subject but kept losing my train of thought; the reefers today are so much stronger than they were in the 1960s. It's like, well, you know, kinda cool, if hard to concen — uh, conc . . . well, to focus. Hehehehehe.

The differences in attitude toward drugs between our two great nations can be summed up in a single profound line, one that puts me into a paroxysm of giggles: Canada *treats* its drug abusers; the United States *punishes* its drug abusers. Think about that for a few seconds, or hours if you will, while you bogart that joint, even though I've begged you not to. Canada recognizes that taking illegal drugs is a serious problem that could lead to AIDS, especially when needles are shared, or even a great high; fear of the latter, in fact, appears to be what Americans experience far more than the former. So, while Canadian officials have set up a "safer injection site" in the popular and romantic

Downtown Eastside of Vancouver, a site that police allow to operate, American law officials simply arrest addicts, lock them up, and throw away the keys. Back north in Canada, a registered nurse dispenses fresh needles, swabs, and sterile water to cook the drugs, along with advice on how to keep the veins healthy — certainly better treatment than my mother-in-law got at a Toronto hospital recently; maybe she's taking the wrong drugs. In Yankee prisons, thank heavens, drugs are far easier to obtain, which may well suggest a certain generosity on the part of Americans.

In the world of heroin, then, Canadians emphasize treatment and education over enforcement crackdowns; Americans, on the other hand, know that a shoot-'em-up movie (pun intended) showing treatment and education would be incredibly tedious, while a movie showing the tracking down and shooting of drug pushers and addicts has far greater potential for colourful explosions and over-turned cars. And it cannot be denied: whose movies make more money — those of Atom Egoyan or those of Yankee directors fresh from making music videos for MTV?

Then there is marijuana, becoming decriminalized in Canada while I struggle to type these words — well, at least possession of small amounts, which is usually enough for me. Americans are furious about even a *partial* decriminalization of "soft drugs" in Canada since it may lead to an increase in a non-taxable type of cross-border shopping. Canada is also "ahead" in legalizing the use of marijuana for medical purposes, unlike the United States, which would rather see AIDS sufferers die in pain; they have had enough good times, apparently, in the process of picking up the illness, and the

Americans do not wish to give them any more. John Ashcroft, the attorney general of the United States, who is religiously sensitive enough to begin every meeting in Washington, DC, with Christian prayers, regardless of the religious leanings of any of his doomed-to-eternal-damnation assistants, knows just how evil homosexuality is since the Bible Told Him So, and he does not choose to reward the occasional result of such actions by doling out free marijuana. Not so Canada, which thinks that it is the government's duty to help its suffering citizens to get high so that they won't get too low. And if that demands the publicly sponsored growing of Kanata Gold, then so be it. The pursuit of "life, liberty, and happiness" in the United States clearly does not include illicit drugs of any kind.

Indeed, while most Canadians have strong doubts about their federal politicians' honesty and competency, at least their elected officials tend to accept the desires of the public. Americans, on the other hand, have a federal government far less likely to liberalize anything at all. So, while nearly four of five Americans believe that marijuana should be legally available as a medicine, and every state ballot initiative on this issue has won, the Bush administration still says no. Indeed, after endless scientific studies and a general consensus that needle exchange reduces HIV or AIDS, George Bush and his Christian Ayatollahs disagree and even mock what is going on in Vancouver. The American government is not unaware that "cannabis" and "Canada" sound suspiciously alike.

Certainly, an argument can be made for the American viewpoint: with a population of but 5% of the world, the United States has 25% of the world's prison population, including nearly 500,000 locked up for violating minor drug laws (that number being larger than the number of prisoners every Western European country has locked up for *any* crime). Apparently, prisons — along with their guards, parole officers, and caterers — are a growth industry in the United States, while Canada is falling seriously behind. Sadly, Canada fell behind its neighbour in the enforcement of the prohibition of alcohol nearly three-quarters of a century ago, which led to the rise of the Bronfman dynasty if nothing else.

Ultimately, Canadians defer less to authority than Americans in spite of what most people think about the purported "passionate individualism" of the latter. For instance, most Americans believe that it is "unpatriotic" to question their leaders, especially during wartime. (Which, thanks to U.S. foreign policy, is pretty well all the time.) Canadians, on the other hand, not only question their leaders constantly but are also forever berating themselves for "voting for those idiots."

Furthermore, Canadians are profoundly modest — justifiably so in the minds of most Americans. Only about one in seven Canadians is eager to "demonstrate superiority" over the rest of the world, while nearly one in three Americans feels the same way. But then, as the Good Book says, "you can influence other people more with a smile and a gun than with a smile alone." (True, this loses something in the translation from the original Aramaic.)

Canadians have an official opposition built into their federal government, which usually means "anyone who is not in the Liberal Party." Americans really have no opposition at all, especially during wartime (see above). After all, as ten thousand U.S. journalists have noted several million times since September 11, 2001, "If you question anything our leaders say, including the arrest without warrant of tens of thousands of suspicious-looking, dark-skinned people with moustaches, you're letting the terrorists win." And they sure as hell wouldn't want that.

A further example of Canadian-American divergence of opinion lies in the decision in the spring of 2003 by the federal government in Ottawa not to appeal an Ontario court ruling that lifted a ban on same-sex marriages. In other words, while Americans firmly believe in the "pursuit" of "happiness," being gay is quite another matter. Americans continue to find it important that homosexuals stay in the closet, but Canadians are clearly happy to decorate the closet and even cater to it. In the country to the north, "the love that dare not speak its name" won't ever shut up; not so in the United States, where it is urged "not to tell," especially in the Armed Forces. But what probably really irks Yankees is that Niagara Falls, Ontario, is far more a honeymoon centre than Niagara Falls, New York. And, of course, American divorce lawyers are now noting all the gay marriages taking place in Canada and drooling in jealousy.

Perhaps this is a good place to list some of the key differences between our two great nations . . . well, between the Great American Empire and the Middling Canadian Umpire.

THE UNITED STATES ON TERRORISM: It must be destroyed.
CANADA ON TERRORISM: It must be debated to death.

THE UNITED STATES ON THE REST OF THE WORLD: They hate us because they are jealous.

CANADA ON THE REST OF THE WORLD: Why doesn't anyone notice that we're here? I mean, like, we're big and nice and cuddly.

THE UNITED STATES ON BIN LADEN: The monster must be stopped.

CANADA ON BIN LADEN: Thank God he mentioned us, along with other countries, as a country that's worthy of being attacked.

THE UNITED STATES ON FIREARMS: Everyone should have a gun, even our children.

CANADA ON FIREARMS: With just a few more billion dollars, our federal government will be able to register hundreds of guns.

THE UNITED STATES ON QUEBEC SEPARATISM: What the hell is Quebec separatism?

CANADA ON QUEBEC SEPARATISM: Quelle d'enfer est separatism du Québec?

THE UNITED STATES ON THE END OF THE WORLD: Nearly one in five believes that "the end of the world" will come during his or her lifetime, and nearly six in ten think that the eschatology described in the Book of Revelation is literally true and will someday occur.

CANADA ON THE END OF THE WORLD: About one in twenty thinks that "the end of the world" will come during his or her lifetime, probably thanks to American foreign policy. And where can we buy this Revelation book? Is it the latest in the Harry Potter series?

AMERICANS ON WHO IS THE "MASTER" IN THE HOME: Almost half of all Americans — 49% — agree with the following: "The father of the family must be master in his own home." Wait till Dagwood hears about this.

CANADIANS ON WHO IS THE "MASTER" IN THE HOME: Fewer than one in five Canadians — 18%, to be exact — thinks that "father knows best." Indeed, often there are two fathers, and, besides, look how laughable Homer Simpson is.

AMERICANS ON HEALTH CARE, SAFETY, AND THE ENVIRONMENT: It's every man for himself, and women are okay too providing that they listen to their masters' voices.

CANADIANS ON HEALTH CARE, SAFETY, AND THE ENVIRONMENT: If the corridors in the hospitals were brightened up a little with happier colours, we'd be willing to wait a few more weeks on the gurneys for our eventual operations; hell, they're free.

AMERICANS ON IMMIGRATION: As long as they're white and Christian and speak English and willing to help raise our kids while receiving less than the minimum wage, everyone is welcome.

CANADIANS ON IMMIGRATION: All are welcome since there is lots of room for everyone, but if husbands insist on those burkas for their wives could they be see through at least?

AMERICANS ON THE DUTY OF GOVERNMENT: It should be a watchdog to make sure that we don't kill each other, unless it's with legal firearms.

CANADIANS ON THE DUTY OF GOVERNMENT: It should be a partner with the private sector and a protector of its citizens, even if we must pay thousands of dollars annually toward some kind of armed forces.

AMERICANS ON WHAT THEY EXPECT FROM THEIR LEADERS: They should enforce the law and catch cheaters, unless they are really important CEOs or really hard-to-catch foreign leaders like that Saddam character, who was behind 9/11, I think. Wasn't he?

CANADIANS ON WHAT THEY EXPECT FROM THEIR LEADERS: They should always be ready and eager and able to step in and find my uncle Louis a job so that the bastard will be able to finally move out and leave us alone.

AMERICANS ON INEQUALITY: Inequality is your own fault. Why didn't your parents leave you a large business to run, a huge house, and a fat stock portfolio like mine did?

CANADIANS ON INEQUALITY: We believe in a sense of community — a community of communities, in fact, even though it sounded funny when Joe Clark said it — and we're not happy when some people are too goddamn rich; let's tax those bastards to death. Who do they think they are, anyway? Americans?

AMERICANS ON POWER: We don't need anybody else. We are the most powerful nation since Ancient Rome and nineteenth-century Great Britain — put together. We are a rock; we are an island. And a rock feels no pain, and an island never cries. (Thanks, Google, and thanks, Paul Simon; the royalties are in the mail.)

CANADIANS ON POWER: We are team players. We are bridge builders. Anyone want to play bridge? We're willing to be the dummy, as usual. And, besides, we don't like war; someone might get hurt. But we lack bullets, anyway.

AMERICANS ON THEIR GREATEST CITY: New York is the best, the biggest, the loudest, the most cultured, the most dangerous. It's the city that never sleeps, showers, or shaves. If we can make it here, we can make it anywhere — and we did, and we do. If you can't take the heat, get off our concrete, you fuckingassholeupyours.

CANADIANS ON THEIR GREATEST CITY: Over 40% of Torontonians come from somewhere else, and 84.6% of them still root for their "home teams" over Canadian ones when they play there. Why, even our diseases come from other continents. We have over two thousand ethnic restaurants, not that we needed any of them to remind us that British cuisine tastes like dreck. Our local radio and TV stations broadcast in nearly three dozen languages, including Patois, Tagalog, and CBC, all of them left-wing. Come see our Sikh temples, our Muslim mosques, our Hindu shrines, our Jewish synagogues, our empty churches. Come see the Danforth, with its Greek signs; our five Chinatowns, with their Chinese signs; the Beaches, with its now-faded signs of "No Irish Need Apply" and "No Jews or Dogs Allowed." And it's the safest city on Earth if you avoid our SARS-ridden hospitals, our West Nile-ridden mosquitoes, beef from western Canada, and any nonethnic restaurants. International terrorists don't even know we exist, and those thousands of terrorists who live here love it too much to blow up anything; it's just like home, only better.

AMERICANS ON THEIR LEADER, GEORGE W. BUSH: God, but he looked manly arriving on that fighter jet in that cooooool combat suit! Sure, he avoided the army as a kid, but he beat the hell out of the sixteenth-century army of Iraq, didn't he? Yeah, he wasn't really elected, but he's kinda cute, and that recent tax cut will allow me to get those Jaguar and Mercedes SUVs I've been longing for.

CANADIANS ON THEIR ETERNAL RULER, JEAN CHRÉTIEN: I can't understand a goddamn word he says, but who cares? He kept us out of Iraq, didn't he? At least he doesn't come to news conferences on a seadoo in a wetsuit, like that western jerk. Sure, he didn't have to take two full years to retire, but then the Lord created the world in only six days, and look at the crappy shape of the world.

AMERICANS ON CANADA AND CANADIANS: Never heard of it. Never heard of them. Are they European?

CANADIANS ON AMERICA AND AMERICANS: What a country! What a people! To think they were once European!

AMERICA IN A PHRASE: "Life, liberty, and the pursuit of happiness," even if I have to kill you to get all three. And I will; I will; I will.

CANADA IN A PHRASE: "Peace, order, and good government"; well, peace and order are still two out of three, and batting even .300 will earn you $5 million (U.S.!) in professional baseball. Remember that.

AMERICA IN A WORD: Passion.
CANADA IN A WORD: Compassion. Well, unless it's gonna cost a lot.

As you can see, even though Canada and the United States lie next to each other, it's pretty clear who lies on top and who lies most of all.

True, the United States managed to get Iceland and the Solomon Islands to join it in the "coalition of the willing" to take on Iraq in the spring of 2003, but then Canada was in pretty good company too in its refusal to attack that duly elected man: Angola, Cameroon, Chile, and Guinea also didn't give a damn about Saddam.

True, all nineteen of the terrorists who attacked the World Trade Center and the Pentagon on 9/11 (or, as Canadians irritatingly call it, "11/9") were legal residents of the United States. But all Americans know in their pure hearts that, had those evil men been legal residents of Canada, they would have had no trouble whatsoever in entering the United States had they chosen to during that fateful time. Today they would get caught up in traffic jams of gay marriage parties in Niagara Falls, Ontario, and lose valuable time as Canadian border guards offer to sell them cheap marijuana, leading to some pretty dangerous driving by many of the future mass murderers down the New York turnpike. And with those far cheaper prescription drugs available in Canada, we can thank our lucky stars that none of the terrorists travelled up here to take advantage of that.

Yes, Canadians purchased $300 billion worth of goods and services from the United States in 2002, but then Americans purchased $380 billion worth of goods and services from us, which must really piss the Yanks off. Thank heavens the Americans lust after our oil, gas, hydro power, and fresh water, all of which could be horribly contaminated if they were to use nuclear weapons against Canada. So maybe there is a God after all, even if most Canadians don't believe in him/her/it/whatever.

This all returns us to the question stated so sweetly and lovingly at the opening of this book: is it better to be a Canadian or an American? If you're really sick, it's far better to be a Canadian because of the free medical care. Well, that is, if you have the money to jump the queue or fly down to the United States for faster medical treatment. Let's try that again: is it better to be a Canadian or an American? It's a decision that has vexed millions over the years, from Mary Pickford to Raymond Burr, from Lorne Greene to Michael J. Fox, from Peter Jennings to Mike Myers to Jim Carrey, and it certainly troubles many of us today.

Let's attempt an answer to this question at last. If you live in Canada, you can always try to make it in the United States. Now how many Americans feel the same way about making it up here? Huh? Think about that. Clearly, Canadians have never lost the American Dream, while the poor Yankees are too dull or spiritually impoverished to even have a Canadian one. It's sad, even pathetic, but true.

I think the answer is clear. And now that I'm finally done with this book, I can get back to watching CNN. If only Canada had a national news network, I swear that I'd watch it. Really.

Allan Gould (here in Toronto, not his native Detroit),

summer 2003

Printed and bound
in Boucherville, Quebec, Canada by
MARC VEILLEUX IMPRIMEUR INC.
in October, 2003